WHY DON'T I DO THE THINGS I KNOW ARE GOOD FOR ME?

BJ GALLAGHER

WHY DON'T I DO THE THINGS I KNOW ARE GOOD FOR ME?

TAKING SMALL STEPS
TOWARD IMPROVING THE BIG PICTURE

BERKLEY BOOKS
NEW YORK

THE BERKLEY PUBLISHING GROUP
Published by the Penguin Group
Penguin Group (USA) Inc.
375 Hudson Street, New York, New York 10014, USA
Penguin Group (Canada), 90 Eglinton Avenue East, Suite 700, Toronto, Ontario M4P 2Y3, Canada (a division of Pearson Penguin Canada Inc.) • Penguin Books Ltd., 80 Strand, London WC2R 0RL, England • Penguin Group Ireland, 25 St. Stephen's Green, Dublin 2, Ireland (a division of Penguin Books Ltd.) • Penguin Group (Australia), 250 Camberwell Road, Camberwell, Victoria 3124, Australia (a division of Pearson Australia Group Pty. Ltd.) • Penguin Books India Pvt. Ltd., 11 Community Centre, Panchsheel Park, New Delhi—110 017, India • Penguin Group (NZ), 67 Apollo Drive, Rosedale, North Shore 0632, New Zealand (a division of Pearson New Zealand Ltd.) • Penguin Books (South Africa) (Pty.) Ltd., 24 Sturdee Avenue, Rosebank, Johannesburg 2196, South Africa

Penguin Books Ltd., Registered Offices: 80 Strand, London WC2R 0RL, England

This book is an original publication of The Berkley Publishing Group.

Cover photos: "Mixed Fruit" by Denis Maranink/Shutterstock Images. "Staircase" by Imagewerks/Getty Images.
Cover design by Annette Fiore DeFex.
Interior text design by Pauline Neuwirth, Neuwirth and Associates, Inc.

PRINTING HISTORY
Berkley trade paperback edition / June 2009

Library of Congress Cataloging-in-Publication Data

Hateley, BJ Gallagher (Barbara J. Gallagher), 1949–
Why don't I do the things I know are good for me? : taking small steps toward improving the big picture / BJ Gallagher
p. cm.
ISBN 978-0-425-21965-2
1. Self-control. 2. Self-management. 3. Positive psychology. I. Title.
BF632.H27 2009
158.1—dc22 2009000924

PRINTED IN THE UNITED STATES OF AMERICA

10 9 8 7 6 5 4 3 2 1

For all the world's women and girls,
with love and laughter

ACKNOWLEDGMENTS

MOST PEOPLE THINK that writing is a solo endeavor, but they are mistaken. Writing a successful book is a group project. It depends upon the talent, skill, insight, creativity, energy, and experience of many people—editors, agents, copyeditors, book designers, marketing professionals—not to mention the friends and family of the author. I am grateful to all the wonderful people who contributed generously to the writing, editing, production, and marketing of this book.

Jill Marsal, my literary agent, helped me in so many ways—encouraging me every step of the way, from initial idea to finished manuscript. Her patience, professionalism, and perseverance impressed me enormously. Her colleagues at the Sandra Dijkstra Agency all played their roles as well, and I am grateful to them.

My editors at Berkley Books, Denise Silvestro and Shannon Jamieson Vazquez, were terrific. I am always thrilled to work with good editors who push, query, challenge, and ask me tough questions—and in the process, force me to become a better writer. Thank you, Denise and Shannon. And thanks to Meredith Giordan for serving as a superb author liaison.

Laine Proctor, my research assistant, contributed statistics to help illustrate key points in the book. It's good to have a great assistant.

My friend Judith Dancoff played a critical role in getting me off the dime to start writing. Judith, I am grateful for your gentle nudging (or was it a kick in the butt?)—and I hope my readers are, too. This book wouldn't exist without you.

My friend Sam Beasley is the person to whom I am most grateful. Sam, you are my wise coach, my generous friend, my practical go-to guy, and my beloved teacher. What would I do without you in my life?

Thank you to the hundreds of friends and colleagues, teachers and preachers, mentors and role models, family members and loved ones who have provided me with both inspiration and instruction over the years. I hope that in sharing some of the lessons you taught me, I have done justice to your pearls of wisdom.

And to the One who gave me the gifts of writing and teaching, I bow my head and whisper simply, "Thanks."

CONTENTS

INTRODUCTION xv
THE GAP BETWEEN WHAT I KNOW AND WHAT I DO

SECTION I. WHY? 1
WHY DON'T I DO WHAT I KNOW IS GOOD FOR ME?

1. Immediate relief from stress or pain is often more compelling than our rational self-interest. 5
2. Childhood conditioning keeps us trapped; low or erratic self-esteem plagues us. 10
3. Good self-care is not fun, interesting, engaging, or tasty. It's boring and bland—who wants that? 15
4. Advertising, marketing, and the media undermine our self-esteem and self-confidence. 18
5. The historical/cultural role of women in the world gives us second-class status, making it difficult to feel good about ourselves. 25
6. Addictions (overeating, shopping, alcohol, pills, men, work, etc.) keep us stuck—unable to do what's good for us. 33

7. Some of us suffer from depression. It's hard to take good care of yourself when you feel like sh★t. 40

SECTION II. HOW? 45
HOW CAN WE CHANGE OUR HABITS OF SELF-CARE?

1. First, just notice what you do and what you don't do. Don't try to change anything—just notice. 51
2. Pay attention to the words you use—in self-talk and in conversations with others. 54
3. Give up the struggle. Make peace with who you are today. 57
4. Don't let what you *can't* do stop you from what you *can* do. 60
5. Catch yourself doing something right (or approximately right). Then pat yourself on the back for it. 62
6. Self-care doesn't mean *selfish*. 65
7. *Help* is not a four-letter word. Get support from others. No one can do it for you, but you can't do it alone. 68
8. Let go of perfectionism—it's both a cause and a result of low self-esteem. 72
9. Fake it 'til you make it. Act as if you value yourself, even when you don't feel like it. 75
10. What would radical self-care look like for you right now? 78
11. Make a gratitude list and build from there. What you focus on is what you'll get more of. 81

12. Clear away negative emotions: worry, fear, anxiety, regret, pessimism. 85

13. Don't "should" on yourself. Drop the words "should" and "ought" from your vocabulary. 88

14. Go to bed half an hour earlier. Self-care begins with the basics. 91

15. Look for women who have what you want and learn from them. 94

16. Practice esteem-able acts. 97

17. Lighten up and laugh . . . a lot. 99

18. Go on a media fast. Be very careful what you put in your head. 101

19. Stop playing the comparison game. 105

20. Draw on spiritual resources to assist you. 108

21. Adopt a flexible notion of self-care; allow it to change over time. 110

22. Ask your friends what they love about you. 112

23. Practice using affirmations to retrain your thinking and your attitude. 115

24. Make self-care into a game. Make it fun, engaging, interesting. 119

25. Do something physical today. Anything. Get your body moving. 122

26. Resting is *not* "doing nothing." 125

27. Forgive people who have hurt you. Forgiving them frees *you*. 127

28. Balance your checkbook. 130

29. It's not what you're eating—it's what's eating you. 133

30. Give up the need to be liked by everyone. 137

31. Never pass up an opportunity to pee. 141

32. Ask yourself, "What's the best use of my time right now?" 143

33. Clean out one drawer or one closet. 146

34. Make appointments with yourself. 149

35. Honor your feelings, but don't be a slave to them. 152

36. Don't go to a dry well for water. Seek out the right people to support you in caring for yourself. 155

37. Put your credit cards in a jar of water and freeze them. 158

38. Wash a window or two in your home or apartment. 161

39. Write down everything you spend this week. Yes, every single penny. 164

40. Meditate for at least five minutes each day. 167

41. Buy yourself some fresh-cut flowers. 171

42. Seek forgiveness from people you've hurt or harmed. Make amends. 173

43. Take care of your car. 176

44. Buy or make a first aid kit. 179

45. Tell yourself the truth about the men in your life. 183

46. Acknowledge all the different ways you avoid doing the things you know are good for you. 187

47. If you, or someone you love, is struggling with an addiction, find a local support group. 190

48. Make a God box. 194

49. Do what you love. 198

50. Enroll in a personal development class. 200

51. Use the phrase "Up until now . . ." to create openings for change. 203

52. Own your accomplishments. Enjoy the "new you" you're becoming. 206

SECTION III. WHAT? 209
WHAT BRINGS ABOUT SUCCESSFUL, LONG-TERM, PERSONAL CHANGE?

1. Learn how your mind works, then put it to work for your highest and best good. 213

2. Study how people bring about positive changes in their lives. 221

3. Coax yourself through the "I don't wanna" feelings. 229

4. Pay attention to the power of your words. 234

5. Stick with the winners. Surround yourself with the right people. 240

6. Teach others how to do the things they know are good for them. 244

CONCLUSION 249
CLOSING THE GAP

INTRODUCTION

THE GAP BETWEEN WHAT I KNOW AND WHAT I DO

A problem cannot be solved at the same level of consciousness that created it.

—Albert Einstein, physicist, Nobel laureate

MILLIONS OF WOMEN struggle with the problem of inadequate self-care—not taking very good care of ourselves. We know the things we *should* do, but we don't do them. There is a huge gap between what we know and what we do. This book is about that gap.

Our problem surely isn't lack of information—bookstores are stocked with hundreds of volumes outlining how to eat less and exercise more; dozens of experts advise us to sock more money away into savings; many wise people warn us we would be better off staying away from troublesome or dangerous relationships. We have plenty of information on getting rid of clutter, organizing time, taking care of our bodies, managing our finances, fulfilling our career dreams. But for some reason, we often don't act on what we know.

In fact, sometimes we do just the opposite of what we know to be in our own best interests. We overeat and underexercise; we spend every last nickel (sometimes more); we fall in love with bad boys and marry inappropriate men (often again and again). We accumulate too much stuff, procrastinate and fritter away time, neglect our bodies, mismanage our money, and bail out on ourselves in countless ways.

What causes us to behave contrary to our own best interests, despite the fact that we know better? Why do smart women do such dumb things when it comes to what's good for us? What makes it so hard for us to take care of ourselves? And why on earth do we put everyone else's needs ahead of our own? As my friend Brenda Knight laments, "Why am I always riding in the back of my own bus?"

The slender volume you hold in your hands has answers to those questions . . . maybe not *all* the answers, nor the *definitive* answers, but big chunks of practical, useful, wise, enlightening answers to the question "Why don't I do the things I know are good for me?" There are enough answers here to jump-start you on the path to active self-care and healthy self-love.

If you take this book seriously—and take yourself seriously—you can begin to practice *the power of positive doing*. We've all heard of the power of positive thinking—my goal is to help you take the next step and get into action, no matter what you're thinking. By taking action, you will move yourself from the back of the bus . . . up front to the driver's seat where you belong.

SECTION I

WHY?

WHY DON'T I DO WHAT I KNOW IS GOOD FOR ME?

Understanding the Source(s) of the Problem

I don't understand myself. I want to do what is right
but I do not do it. Instead, I do the very thing I hate. . . .
It seems to be a fact of life that when I want to do
what's right, I inevitably do what's wrong.

—Romans 7:15–19

THERE ISN'T ONE simple answer to the question "Why don't I do the things I know are good for me?" The factors that affect our self-care behavior are many—cultural, familial, psychological, spiritual/religious, emotional, economic, and historical. I have interviewed hundreds of women, read dozens of research studies, and talked to a variety of experts who, not surprisingly, had a variety of answers.

Their answers fall into two categories—*external* reasons for not doing what you know is good for you, and *internal* reasons. For most women, it's a combination of both.

For instance, I may cite "a desire for immediate comfort and stress relief" as an internal reason for eating junk food, but I may also mention the influence of a role model (external reason), in that "I saw my mother comfort herself with food." Internal feelings are often supported by external influences—making it especially difficult to break out of old habits and develop new, positive self-care routines.

You may read this book in any order that suits you. It was written in such a way that the chapters flow organically from one to the next, but that's not to say that you must read them in order. Read them and work with them in a way that makes sense to you. If a specific issue resonates with you or you feel drawn to it, by all means, feel free to start there. What matters most is not *where* you start, but *that* you start.

A few questions at the end of each chapter are designed to help you reflect on your own barriers to self-care. Think about the questions—ask yourself what gets in *your* way when you don't do what you know is good for you. Make some notes in response to the questions, or write in the margins of the pages. The more you *do* with this book—rather than just *reading* it—the more you will get out of it.

CHAPTER 1

IMMEDIATE RELIEF FROM STRESS OR PAIN IS OFTEN MORE COMPELLING THAN OUR RATIONAL SELF-INTEREST.

I try to fill the emptiness deep inside me with Cheetos,
but I am still depressed.
Only now my fingers are stained orange.
I am blue. And I am orange.

—Karen Salmansohn, author of *How to Be Happy, Dammit*

THE GAP BETWEEN what we know and what we do is not a new problem—it's probably as old as human nature itself. We human beings are complex creatures—paradoxical, contradictory, multifaceted, multilayered, and often quite confusing . . . especially to ourselves.

We're clearly not very rational creatures—we do so many things that are not in our rational self-interest. I think human beings are like M&M's: We have a thin veneer of rationality on the outside, but if you scratch the surface, inside we are a rich, dark mass of instincts, feelings, and emotional impulses. Our rationality is vastly overrated—it's our nonrational nature that really runs the show.

This is especially true when it comes to doing the things we know are good for us. Our self-care behavior is often not based in rationality—it's based in our instincts and emotions. If we feel anxious or fearful, we know that spending some time meditating, taking a long walk, or calling a close friend would be good self-care, but instead we reach for ice cream or candy bars to soothe ourselves. We know we should prepare healthy meals, but we feel too busy to cook, so instead we grab some fast food and eat on the go. We know we should be saving money for the house that we want to buy someday, but instead we fritter away our money on impulse purchases. We know we should go to the gym, but at the end of the day we're just too tired, so instead we tune out the stress of the day by zoning out in front of the TV. The examples are endless.

Our rational thoughts may tell us what would be good for us, but our fatigue and emotions—the need for immediate stress relief or comfort—override our rationality. It's not because of weakness—this isn't a character flaw of some kind. It's because we're human, and we humans will opt for immediate relief of pain in almost every situation.

All living organisms move *toward* pleasure and *away* from pain. It is a basic law of nature. It's a healthy instinct to react to pain by seeking to escape it. This is true even for a one-celled organism: stick an amoeba with a pin or apply heat, and it will pull away. It's the same with complex organisms—it is normal to seek relief from pain. Only a masochist says, "Oh, pain, this is good." The rest of us automatically look for some way to stop the pain—and as quickly as possible *ifyouplease!* Physical pain, emotional pain, psychological pain, spiritual pain, economic pain—it doesn't matter. When we feel pain, we will instinctively look for the quickest, easiest way to make the pain go away. There is nothing wrong or weird about it. Seeking relief is a normal, healthy, appropriate response. If you *didn't* seek pain relief, you'd be weird!

Reaching for short-term pain relief isn't necessarily always a problem—it's only a problem when it works against your long-term welfare. Your desire for the comfort of chocolate today keeps you from losing the weight you want to lose for the sake of your health and appearance. Your "need" to have those darling shoes means less money in your new-car fund. Your discomfort with the idea that someone's feelings might get hurt keeps you in a relationship with a person whom you don't care to be friends with anymore. I could list pages of examples—and so could you.

Allowing short-term or immediate concerns to outweigh our own long-term self-interest is probably the single biggest reason we often don't do what we know is good for us. It's a never-ending struggle. And Now wins out over Tomorrow almost every day of the week. You're not alone—millions of us do the same thing. Don't beat yourself up. For now, just notice it when it comes up for you, and we'll get into solutions in the second and third sections of this book.

• Begin by Just Noticing •

SOMETHING THAT is good for us often speaks in the voice of "I should." I should: go to bed earlier, get more exercise, save more money, say "no thanks" to my in-laws' invitation to go home for the holidays, etc. Listen to the "I should" that comes up for you in various situations. The "I should" is coming from your head—it is the voice of reason. (Although sometimes the "I should" is irrational, too—we'll get to that a little later.) It is the rational adult part of you that does, indeed, know what is good for you.

Now, listen to the voice that usually wins out—it speaks as "I want" or "I need." I need: a drink, a reward, a little treat, an escape, a pick-me-up, a new outfit for my date, etc. "I want" and "I need" come from your feelings—the nonrational part of you. You feel your wants and needs in your body, your heart, your soul, or your stomach. It feels urgent, strong, irresistible. Is it any wonder that "I want" and "I need" win out over "I should"? Wants and needs are very compelling—telling you what would bring you relief (or pleasure) *right now*.

Make notes to yourself as you think about these questions:

When does "I should" come up for you? Are there certain times of day or specific situations that trigger an "I should"?

And when does "I want" or "I need" drive your behavior? When does the longing for relief or comfort make you do things that you know aren't good for you?

In what situations do you most strongly feel the tug-of-war between "I should" and "I need/want"? How do you feel during that struggle?

CHAPTER 2

CHILDHOOD CONDITIONING KEEPS US TRAPPED; LOW OR ERRATIC SELF-ESTEEM PLAGUES US.

Childhood is the first, inescapable political situation
each of us has to negotiate. You are powerless.
You are on the wrong side in every respect.
Besides that, there's the size thing.

—June Jordan, poet, essayist, activist

"WHAT'S THE MATTER with you? Can't you do anything right?" my father snapped at me as we walked up the steps to the courthouse. I had stumbled, almost falling. I was sixteen at the time, and we had to go to court because I had been at fault in a fender bender. He was angry with me, understandably. But it felt like more than anger. It was a deep, intense resentment about my behavior reflecting badly on him. I can still feel the white-hot harshness of his words. I didn't need a judge to pronounce me guilty—my father had already done it. His words felt like the bullets of a verbal firing squad. My spirit died a little that morning on the courthouse steps—one of many little "deaths" I was to experience in childhood.

If you grew up in a home where there was no verbal, emotional, or physical abuse, count yourself *very* lucky—you are one of the rare women who enjoyed a childhood free from painful wounding and scars.

The vast majority of us had parents who meant well, but whose poor insight or empathy, emotional deformities, and/or demons of their own kept them from being the kind of loving, supportive caretakers that children need. We survived as best as we could as kids, and we seem to spend the rest of our lives recovering from childhood. For some, recovery is difficult to achieve, for the wounds are deep and the scars impenetrable.

What were the messages you received as a child? Did you feel stupid, homely, unloved, unacceptable in some way? Did you fail to measure up to your parents' expectations? Or were you the favorite child? Daddy's little girl? What messages about yourself did you pick up at school? Were you one of the popular girls, and how did that shape your self-image? Or did you feel left out of the in-group, and how did that shape your sense of self today? Did any religious teachers influence how you felt about yourself? How did their ideas influence who you are as an adult?

Childhood influences are extremely powerful. Our caretakers—parents, teachers, and others—gave us thousands of messages about who we were and what they thought of us. It is impossible for a child not to believe these messages and internalize them.

Self-esteem problems are the most common result of negative programming in childhood. Little girls who are criticized, shamed, nagged, harassed, and neglected—especially by their fathers—are highly likely to grow up with low or erratic self-esteem. A study in the *Canadian Journal of Human Sexuality* reported that "women's perception of their father's unconditional regard [or lack of it] was significantly related to self-esteem."*

A girl who feels unloved, unappreciated, unaccepted as a kid will almost always grow into a woman who doesn't feel good about herself. It shows up in myriad ways—insecurity, anxiety, poor posture, eating disorders, lack of self-confidence in social or work situations, attraction to men who will continue to put her down or abuse her, and more. Poor self-esteem due to lack of good parenting is one of the chief reasons women cite for not taking care of themselves.

It makes sense. We take good care of the things we love. But if we don't love something (or someone), we don't take care of it. We neglect it. We ignore it. We discount it.

---

* Richards, Maryse H., Idy B. Gitelson, Anne C. Petersen, and Anita L. Hurtig. "Adolescent Personality in Girls and Boys: The Role of Mothers and Fathers." *Psychology of Women Quarterly* 15, (1991): 65–81. As cited in Scheffler, Tanya S. and Peter J. Naus. "The Relationship Between Fatherly Affirmation and a Woman's Self-Esteem, Fear of Intimacy, Comfort with Womanhood and Comfort with Sexuality." *The Canadian Journal of Human Sexuality* 8, no. 1 (Spring 1999): 39–45.

Poor self-esteem shows up in our conversations. Someone pays us a compliment and we shrug it off: "This old dress? It's nothing special." Someone praises us and we resist the praise, saying, "Oh, it wasn't really a big deal." Or we try to pass the praise off to someone else: "I couldn't have done it without Kayla and Maria—they deserve most of the credit."

My friend Arleen Gevanthor is like that. She is the most amazing jewelry designer I've ever known, coming up with unusual creations designed around colored stones. A Los Angeles gallery recently featured a collection of Arleen's pieces at a high-powered fashion show. Arleen, who's over eighty, wasn't able to attend due to health problems, so after the show I called to tell her how impressed everyone was with her stunning baubles and to inform her that a magazine was interested in doing a spread about her gems. I was bubbling with excitement as I related all the good news. "Oh, shush," she said. "I just can't hear all this." I suddenly realized that she simply couldn't take it in. After growing up with a hypercritical New York Jewish mother, then decades of marriage to a critical husband (any surprise she married *him*?), her self-esteem was so low she just couldn't bear the praise and enthusiasm I was relaying to her. She had to reject it.

Poor self-esteem is rampant among American women today, and influences from childhood are one of the key reasons.

• Begin by Just Noticing •

PAY ATTENTION to how you feel about yourself in all kinds of different situations. When do you feel peaceful and happy? Confident and secure? When do you feel insecure? Worthless? Not good enough? How would you describe your self-esteem? On a scale of one to ten, ten being highest, how would you rate your self-acceptance, self-regard, self-love? Is it consistent all the time, or does it change a lot? When does it go up? When does it go down? Just notice. You don't have to do anything right now. Just notice.

CHAPTER 3

GOOD SELF-CARE IS NOT FUN, INTERESTING, ENGAGING, OR TASTY. IT'S BORING AND BLAND—WHO WANTS THAT?

A waist is a terrible thing to mind.
—Cathy Conheim, therapist, author

NOT ALL THE reasons for poor self-care are deep psychological issues or powerful social/historical influences. Let's face it—one of the primary reasons a lot of us have for not practicing good self-care is much simpler: It's just not fun.

Cathy Conheim, a therapist and author of *A Waist Is a Terrible Thing to Mind*, says that in her therapy practice she sees a lot of little kids trapped in adult bodies. "I'm not sure I know *any* adults," she muses. Maybe she's right. Perhaps there aren't any adults—maybe we're all little kids in big bodies.

And what do kids want to do? To have fun, play games, do interesting things, eat sweets, be creative, go on adventures, dream and fantasize, and enjoy life. Kids don't want to eat broccoli—and neither do we. Cherry Garcia ice cream or mint chocolate chip (my personal fave) is much more attractive. Oreos, Cheez-Its, Cheetos, Froot Loops, pizza, burgers, French fries, and soft drinks (yum!) are much more appealing than salads, vegetables, whole grains, fresh fruit, and water to drink (blech!).

The three things I most dislike doing are balancing my checkbook, grocery shopping, and getting gas at the gas station. Borrrrring. I don't like to do the mundane things of life—things that involve no creativity, challenge, fun, or excitement. I get no satisfaction out of those activities. But they're all aspects of self-care, aren't they? Keeping food in the house, gas in the car, and money in my accounts is part and parcel of taking good care of myself.

If you're like most women, this is one of the reasons your self-care isn't what you'd like it to be. You don't have to be Sigmund Freud to solve this part of your self-care puzzle—all you have to do is look at the Fun Factor. A lot of self-care necessities rate a big fat zero when it comes to fun.

• Begin by Just Noticing •

THINK ABOUT aspects of self-care that you really don't like to do. Maybe it's as simple as washing off your makeup before you go to bed. Perhaps it's drinking water or eating veggies. It could be that the thing you really don't like is exercise . . . or sweating.

Don't try to change anything right away—just notice. What are the thoughts that go through your head when you think about those self-care items? What are your feelings?

Now think about some activities that you really love to do. What feelings come up for you? Do you feel happy or excited when you reflect on those activities? Do any of them make you feel like a kid? Pay attention to these feelings. Becoming aware of who we are and what motivates us is an important first step in overcoming our barriers to great self-care.

CHAPTER 4

ADVERTISING, MARKETING, AND THE MEDIA UNDERMINE OUR SELF-ESTEEM AND SELF-CONFIDENCE.

When Sleeping Beauty wakes up . . .
she is almost fifty years old.
—Maxine Kumin, poet

A NUMBER OF years ago I attended a weekend workshop with Will Schutz, one of the pioneers of the human potential movement at the Esalen Institute in Big Sur, California. It turned out to be the weirdest weekend of my life—in a good way. It was a workshop called "Group Process," but for me it was so much more. Perhaps it had to do with my turning forty that summer—one of those big birthdays that prompts intense self-reflection, reassessment, and a quest for the answer to my question: Is this how I want to spend the rest of my life?

One of the things that Will said that weekend was that deep down inside, every human harbors three fundamental fears—the fear that "I'm incompetent," the fear that "I'm insignificant," and the fear that "I'm unlovable." We spend our lives driven by those fears—worrying that they are true. Whenever anything or anyone comes close to confirming one of those fears, we spring into action, defending ourselves, driving away whoever or whatever threatens to make our worst fear come true. This notion was enormously helpful in my quest to understand myself, in both my personal and my professional life. Why I do the things I do—or don't do—became much clearer. And with new clarity, I could make new choices.

This notion of inner fears is also helpful in understanding the roles that marketing, advertising, and the media play in our lives. In a nutshell: Marketing and advertising professionals know about those three fears at our core. They didn't need to go to Esalen to find out—they've known it for years, decades, perhaps forever. After all, people have been selling stuff to other people almost since the start of time—beginning with primitive barter in the early days, through the invention of money and tokens of trade, and into today's sophisticated advertising and promotion. We lived in a world of global trade even before the time of Christ—when explorers traded tea, spices, silk, and other valuable commodities with other tribes and countries.

And since those early days, women have played an important role, influencing the exchange of goods and services with their taste for exotic foods and valuables that could only be found in distant lands. The men did the traveling and trading, of course, but it was the women who wanted the finest silk, the wonderful spices, and items like sugar, coffee, tobacco, tea, and salt.

Fast-forward a couple thousand years and women's influence on the purse strings hasn't changed much. CNNMoney.com reported in 2004 that "women choose how 88 percent of every disposable dollar is spent—including 53 percent of all stock purchases, 63 percent of personal computer buys, and 75 percent of all over-the-counter drug outlays."*

In the automotive industry—which you'd think would be the guys' bailiwick—women actually buy 56 percent of all cars and trucks each year, and they *influence* over 80 percent of all vehicle purchases. Automotive companies know this, and target their advertising and marketing efforts accordingly. They are not alone. In 2003, the *Arizona Daily Star* reported "a massive increase in advertising dollars spent on ads specifically geared toward women . . . [with] targeted increases specifically in the following markets: automobiles, financial services, and home improvement. . . . Most ads aim to make an 'emotional connection' with women."**

---

* Crawford, Krysten. "Ads for Women Are 'Miss Understood': Recent Study Concludes That Ads Targeting Newly Empowered Women Are Mostly Clichéd and Offensive." CNNMoney.com, September 22, 2004, http://money.cnn.com/2004/09/22/news/midcap/advertising_women/index.htm.

** Mracek, Karen and Shella Jacobs. "More Advertising Is Now Directed at Women Buyers." *The Arizona Daily Star*, November 23, 2003.

If all this is true—and it is—you're probably asking yourself, "Then why do I feel so bad about advertising—ads that are supposedly directed at women like me? Why do I feel exploited? And why don't my purchases make me happy, like the advertising promises?"

Good questions! With more and more ads directed at us, why do we seem to feel worse about ourselves?

Here's at least part of the answer: The CNNMoney .com article also reported that women around the world "are subjected to advertising that is often full of clichés, uninspiring and even offensive . . . 65 percent of women between the ages of 35 and 40 found advertising aimed at women to be patronizing [and] 50 percent of them found these ads to be 'old-fashioned.'" But does the fact that women don't *like* the ads mean that they are *unaffected* by them?

Filmmaker and former magazine editor Jean Kilbourne answers no. "I've been doing research and lecturing on the image of women in advertising since the late 1960s. In 1979 a filmed version of my lecture was made entitled *Killing Us Softly*. These images are still killing us softly, and by 'us' I mean all of us: women, men, and children. I think we know by now the image of women is primarily negative. However, just about everyone has the illusion of being personally exempt from the influence of advertising. So wherever I go what I hear more than anything else is, 'Well, I of course don't pay any attention to ads, I just tune them out. They don't have any effect on me.'"*

The Social Issues Research Centre in Oxford, England, reports that ads on TV and in magazines tend to use the most idealized images of women—research has shown that exposure to these ads negatively impacts body image.** What are we to make of the fact that the average fashion model is 5'9" to 6' tall, while the average American woman is 5'4" tall? The average fashion model weighs 110 to 118 pounds; the average American woman weighs 155 pounds. The average fashion model wears a size 0 or 2; the average American woman wears a size 14.

How do these ultra-skinny models affect the girls who see the ads? The Social Issues Research Centre reports that "more than 80 percent of fourth grade girls have been on a fad diet." HealthAtoZ.com informs us that each year, U.S. consumers spend over $33 billion on "weight-reduction programs, diet foods and beverages." In 1970, the diet industry was a $10 billion industry—today it is a $60 billion industry. On any given day, 48 million Americans are dieting, and you can bet that most of them are women.

But despite the plethora of nutrition and diet books,

---

* Kilbourne, Jean. *Still Killing Us Softly: Advertising's Image of Women*, directed by Margaret Lazarus and Renner Wunderlich (1987).

** Fox, Kate. "Mirror, Mirror: A Summary of Research Findings on Body Image." Social Issues Research Centre, 1197, http://www.sirc.org/publik/mirror.html.

exercise programs, and TV fitness gurus, American women are losing the battle of the bulge. The Institute of Medicine reports that people who lose weight on diets regain two-thirds of the weight they lost within one year, and all of it within five years. Diets don't work—and by now we should know it.

But the advertising machine is relentless. Not only are unrealistically skinny girls hyped as sexy, desirable, and happy, but Madison Avenue is always ready, willing, and able to sell us the latest "secret weapon" to fight fat, whether the weapon is a new food plan or a "magic" exercise machine that promises you a youthful, hard body—in just six weeks, with only fifteen minutes a day—or some other quick and easy program guaranteed to make you beautiful, sexy, fit, and trim, just like the girls and women in the ads. And though women tell Jean Kilbourne that they are unaffected by such ads, the nonstop ka-ching of cash registers all over America tells us the real truth. Because deep down inside, we all harbor those three fears: that we're unlovable, incompetent, and insignificant. And just like the eager folks who purchase magical curative elixirs based on the big promises of snake oil salesmen, we, too, are eager to buy the Next Big Thing promising to make us lovable, competent, and significant.

Marketing and advertising people have got our number. They may not have degrees in psychiatry or psychology, but they understand human nature, especially female nature.

They understand us better than we understand ourselves—and we have no one to blame but ourselves.

The media is not full of evil people trying to make us feel terrible about ourselves or not take good care of ourselves. But the media's piece of the giant puzzle is important to understand. Advertising and marketing people are simply doing their jobs in a capitalist system, which depends upon endless demand for more, bigger, and better goods and services. If we learn to understand ourselves better than they understand us, we can no longer be manipulated.

When we face our own doubts, fears, and insecurities and come to terms with them, this particular barrier to self-care will be easy to avoid.

• Begin by Just Noticing •

KEEP A piece of paper or notepad next to the TV. Every time you watch a program, make a note of the images of women that are portrayed—both in the program and in the commercials that support it.

Do the same when you read women's magazines. Pay close attention to the subliminal messages the ads are trying to convey to you.

You don't need to do anything about it right now—just notice.

CHAPTER 5

THE HISTORICAL/CULTURAL ROLE OF WOMEN IN THE WORLD GIVES US SECOND-CLASS STATUS, MAKING IT DIFFICULT TO FEEL GOOD ABOUT OURSELVES.

Self-esteem isn't everything;
it's just that there's nothing without it.
—Gloria Steinem, feminist pioneer, author,
founding editor of *Ms.* magazine

SOMETIME IN THE 1990s, I went on a business trip to Malaysia. While in Kuala Lumpur, I visited a museum that featured a special exhibition called "Sex." The idea of such an exhibit in a Muslim country intrigued and puzzled me—it seemed a bit oxymoronic from a cultural point of view, if you know what I mean. But, ever the curious sociologist, I had to check out this Sex exhibit, sure that it would be something to write home about.

Malaysian schoolgirls were touring the museum that afternoon, moving through the exhibit in small clusters of six to ten, looking like so many pretty little birds in their pastel head scarves and long garments. I wanted so much to take photos of these innocents peering at the various parts of the Sex exhibit, but couldn't figure out a way to do so without being intrusive and/or rude. So the snapshot exists only in my memory—a study in contrasts.

It was a terrific exhibit—thorough, tasteful, interesting, and educational. Clearly, a multidisciplinary team had put a lot of time and planning into exploring sex from the points of view of history, religion, biology, anthropology, sociology, literature, psychology, and art. I learned a lot that afternoon, and was very happy I'd followed my instincts in going there.

One of the most interesting exhibits explained how, throughout history, men have always had a vested interest in controlling women's sexuality and reproductive capability. There were photos of artifacts from different eras—from chastity belts to veils and scarves, to burkas, and many more items—all designed by men to protect their women from sexual overtures from other men.

As I read what the exhibitors wrote about the issue, it seemed they were implying that humans were not much different from our cousins in the animal kingdom, where a male will go to great lengths to protect his sexual access to a prime female—fighting off competitors, jealously guarding his mate. He's driven by instincts designed to ensure that *his* genes are carried on into future generations. It's a biological imperative—any self-respecting male must protect his genetic legacy by protecting his female(s). The male must be ever vigilant in guarding his mate—for if another male gained access to her, she might bear that male's offspring instead of his own. And no male wants to raise, feed, and care for another male's offspring—it is not in his own interest to do so.

In some species, like lions, competitive males will even kill a lioness's cubs by another male, so that she will go into heat sooner and he can mate with her—producing his own offspring in place of the others. This kind of sexual conquest occurs in other species as well.

We can learn a lot about ourselves by studying the animal kingdom—especially from social animals like lions, wolves, dolphins, elephants, apes, monkeys, and others. Increasingly, scientists are discovering the powerful role that biology plays in human behavior—and the insights they offer can be profoundly helpful in understanding human gender differences, male/female dynamics, and the problems women struggle with in patriarchal societies where males dominate society, politics, economics, culture, and family.

In virtually every culture around the world, women have less status, power, and control over their own lives than men. It makes sense if you remember that for thousands of years, women *were* property! Like livestock, women and children were considered the property of the male head of household.

Even in America, where "we've come a long way, baby," we're still struggling to be seen and treated as equals to men. Prior to 1920, American women were not allowed to vote. And as recently as the 1960s, married women could not hold credit cards in their own name—only their husbands could have credit card accounts.

Throughout history, a man's status depended on wealth, class, and what he did for a living—a woman's status depended on whom she married (or whom she was a mistress to). For all the progress that the women's movement has made, this is still largely true. A woman is valued for her beauty, sensuality, and fertility, while a man is valued for his ability to make money.

In the animal kingdom, a female's chances of survival, and the survival of her young, are greatly enhanced if she is the sexual partner of an alpha male. So it is in the human realm as well—a woman's life is greatly enhanced if she can attract a powerful alpha male. Research indicates that she will live longer, be healthier, enjoy a higher standard of living, and see her children grow into adulthood with a greater chance of success for themselves.

One need only look at divorce statistics to see the harsh truth—when a couple divorces, the man's economic well-being takes a small hit, then he rebounds; the woman's economic well-being, along with her children's, takes a nosedive. And unlike her ex-husband, she does not usually rebound unless she can attract another husband.

I could go on with pages of documentation and research on the second-class status of women around the world. But I'd be preaching to the choir. You already know it, because you live it.

But here's what we sometimes forget—we forget that this is a social problem first, and an individual problem second. Let me explain with a story:

Years ago, in graduate school, I was having a conversation over lunch with an English professor, Bob Beyer. I was complaining about how oppressed I had felt my whole life—first by my domineering father, then by my domineering husband. I was divorced by then, but still felt under the thumb of both men because my dad was giving me money to help me with grad school, and my ex was paying child support. I felt completely dependent on both of them, and resentful of my situation. Dr. Beyer was a sympathetic listener as I related my unhappiness.

Then he asked me a question: "What if you looked at this from a different perspective? Perhaps what you're experiencing is not unique to you. Maybe it's not an individual problem—it's a group problem. I think what you're describing is a sociological issue that affects millions of women. It's not just you."

Wow. That had never occurred to me. It wasn't personal. It was sociological—and economic, and historical, and political, and so forth.

I suddenly felt much better. I'm not sure why. Is it that misery loves company? Or that the "me" problem was now reframed as a "we" problem? I don't know. All I know is that it cheered me up enormously.

Bob and I continued our conversation and his advice to me was brilliant. He said, "Maybe what you need to do is commit some act of independence from your father and your ex. Perhaps you could do something that you know they disapprove of—just to demonstrate that you are your own woman. You can't do anything right now about how *other* women feel oppressed by the men in their lives, but you can do something about your *own* life." He asked me to think about some appropriate act of rebellion.

Since money was the issue for me—my financial dependence on these two men gave them power over me—my act of defiance should have something to do with money. So I bought a coffee table. A lovely square rattan box, with a heavy glass top—simple, elegant, and lovely.

It wasn't exorbitantly expensive—just expensive enough to be out of my budget. And I didn't need a coffee table—I just wanted it. This was a choice, not a necessity.

The day the coffee table was delivered was a marvelous day. I was happy with my newfound spunk and freedom. My dad and my ex knew nothing of my purchase yet, but that didn't matter. I did it for me, and I was happy!

I invited my dad to come over for dinner the following week. This was to be my Big Moment, when my independence would become official. By deliberately eliciting his disapproval, I would set myself free.

I got more and more excited as the days rolled by and my dinner with Dad drew close. Finally the day arrived, and I prepared a lovely meal. I glanced at the clock again and again, counting the hours to the Big Moment.

Then, at the very last minute, I clenched up. About thirty minutes before my father was to arrive, I pulled the glass top off its base, dragged it down the hall, and shoved it under my bed. All that was left was the simple square rattan base.

Dad arrived and of course he noticed the rattan box in front of the sofa. "Is that new?" He frowned.

"Oh, that?" I replied. "No, I've had it in the garage for a while—I got it at a yard sale. I finally decided to bring it in the house and use it."

"Oh," he said, then changed the subject.

This is the challenge we women face. We want to feel good about ourselves—we want to feel equal to men. But to the extent that we are financially dependent on them, we rebel to our own peril. My truth was, I needed my father's support to get through grad school and I couldn't risk his wrath.

I recall a conversation I had with my mother a few years after my aborted coffee-table rebellion. "Why didn't you ever leave Dad?" I asked her. Her marriage was miserable, she was desperately unhappy, and she drowned her pain in bottles of gin. She answered my question with a question. "Where was I supposed to go? I had no college, no skills, no way to make a living—and I had two kids. How could I leave?"

The problem wasn't really Dad—the problem was, and is, the economic realities of gender roles. The other Golden Rule is alive and well: He who has the gold, rules.

Germaine Greer once wrote that a woman must have her own money if she is to be truly her own woman. This is one of the biggest barriers to self-care that women face—not just American women, but women around the world. Our financial dependence on men, the cultural/political/economic realities that we face, make it difficult for us to feel good about ourselves. If we feel inferior to men—and there are plenty of ways our cultures tell us that we're inferior—it's hard to keep caring for ourselves.

• Begin by Just Noticing •

REFLECT ON what you were taught about women's roles in your family, in school while you were growing up, and in church or synagogue. What were some of the "rules" of how women were supposed to behave, in public and in private?

Who controlled the money in your family? Who earned the money? Did anyone inherit money? Did that change the family dynamic in any way? What were you taught to believe about money?

How do your cultural values affect how you care for yourself? Do you believe that it is a virtue for women to put their families first? Why or why not?

You don't need to do anything differently right away—for now, just notice the cultural, social, and financial norms all around you. Pay attention to the messages about expectations, roles, and taboos, especially about women's sexuality.

CHAPTER 6

ADDICTIONS (OVEREATING, SHOPPING, ALCOHOL, PILLS, MEN, WORK, ETC.) KEEP US STUCK—UNABLE TO DO WHAT'S GOOD FOR US.

Reality is for people who can't handle drugs.

—Lily Tomlin, comedian, author, actress

IN HER BOOK *Start Where You Are*, Buddhist nun and author Pema Chödrön relates how she participated in sweat lodges when she was young: "I would always sit by the flap covering the entrance to the sweat lodge. That way, if things got too intense, I could quickly, easily duck out."

In reading her account, I thought, "that's a great metaphor for how people live their lives, especially those who become addicts." Sweat lodges are ceremonial saunas from the Native American tradition, designed to be intensely spiritual and challenging, powerfully moving, cleansing, and healing. It's a hot, sweaty, personal encounter between other people, a shaman or medicine man, and you. I've never been to a sweat lodge, but I can imagine there would be plenty of times I'd want to bolt out the door, too. Spiritual experiences can be very confrontational—like life.

Chödrön says that probably the hardest thing in life is just to live in our own skin. She asserts that most Americans find it almost impossible to just BE—in any given moment, in any given place. We distract ourselves with anything and everything: food, booze, shopping, TV, the Internet, magazines, video games, cell phones, or the iPods plugged into our ears to keep us from being fully present in the moment. We use compulsive work, compulsive exercise, compulsive love affairs—lots of things—to escape from our day-to-day lives.

It is so hard just to be still and be alone with yourself. Most of us will do anything to avoid it. We view being alone as a failure—and sometimes we'll hang out with just about anybody, just to avoid being alone.

For being alone means feeling your feelings: fear, anxiety, happiness, anger, joy, resentment, disappointment, anticipation, sadness, excitement, despair. It doesn't really matter if our feelings are positive or negative—they're exhausting, and we'd just prefer to numb out.

So we duck out the door of our own metaphorical sweat lodge and escape into something—anything—that will make us feel better. If we're down, we seek something to bring us up. If we're up, we seek something to tone it down just a little. We're continually mood-altering, one way or the other.

Sooner or later, we find something that works as an all-purpose drug—a panacea for whatever ails you. For many women, this panacea is food. Refined carbs and sugar, in particular, are the drug of choice for millions of American women.

The NOW Foundation estimates that as many as ten million women and girls suffer from bulimia and/or anorexia, and another twenty million struggle with a binge eating disorder.

Alcohol, too, has been a perennial favorite, leading tobacco, marijuana, cocaine, and pills as the feminine drug of choice. Female alcoholics have death rates that are 50 to 100 percent higher than those of male alcoholics, with more women alcoholics dying from suicide, alcohol-related accidents, cirrhosis of the liver, and circulatory disorders.*

As many as 2.7 million American females older than 12 abuse alcohol and nearly 5 million women reported using an illicit drug at least once in the past month: 3.6 million smoked marijuana; 440,000 indulged in cocaine (one-fourth of them in the form of crack); and nearly 2 million had used an inhalant.**

---

* "Alcohol and Women." *National Institute on Alcohol Abuse and Alcoholism*, no. 10, PH 290, (October 1990).

** Wetherington, Ph.D., Cora Lee, and Adele B. Roman, eds. *Drug Addiction Research and the Health of Women.* Washington, D.C.: U.S. Dept. of Health and Human Services, National Institutes of Health, National Institute on Drug Abuse, 1998.

We joke about women's emotional shopping: "Anybody who thinks that money can't buy love simply doesn't know where to shop," quipped blonde beauty Bo Derek, famous for her movie *10*. But it's no laughing matter. One in twenty American women are compulsive buyers, according to a 2006 study at Stanford University. Lorin Koran, lead author of the study, writes: "Compulsive buying leads to serious psychological, financial, and family problems including depression, overwhelming debt, and the breakup of relationships. People don't realize the extent of damage it does to the sufferer."*

Smoking is still a serious problem among women—the primary reason that many women and girls smoke and are afraid to quit is their fear of gaining weight. These females choose a drug (nicotine) that is clearly a killer, over a less deadly but still harmful drug (sugar). We might die, but we'll look damn good in our coffins!

More than 25 percent of women in the United States smoke cigarettes and increasing numbers are dying of smoking-related illnesses: cancer, cardiovascular disease, and chronic lung disease. In a 2001 report, Surgeon General David Satcher declared: "An epidemic. There is no better word to describe the 600 percent increase since 1950 in women's death rates from lung cancer, a disease primarily

---

* Koran, Lorin M., Ronald J. Faber, Elias Aboujaoude, Michael D. Large, and Richard T. Serpe. "Estimated Prevalence of Compulsive Buying Behavior in the United States." *The American Journal of Psychiatry* 163, (October 2006): 1806–1812.

caused by cigarette smoking." Since 1987, lung cancer has been the leading cancer killer of women—surpassing breast cancer.

Millions of women are in the grip of hidden addictions—fooling themselves and their families into thinking "I'm fine. There's nothing wrong with me. I just need a little something to take the edge off . . . or to help me get through a tough week. A girl is entitled to take her comfort now and then, isn't she?"

But "taking our comfort" costs us dearly. What starts out as a little stress relief or some fun and relaxation soon turns into a habit, which, if ignored, often balloons into a full-blown addiction. Whatever their drug of choice, women from all walks of life, all ages and ethnic backgrounds, are succumbing to the siren song of addiction.

In terms of doing what we know is good for us, using addictive substances (like sugar or cigarettes or alcohol) or engaging in addictive processes (like shopping) are the antithesis of good self-care. The problem is, even when we come out of our denial, we can't quit even if we desperately want to. We're hooked.

Some would say that everybody is hooked on something. Anne Wilson Schaef, in her book *When Society Becomes an Addict*, says that we live in a society that encourages—nay, demands—that you become addicted to *something*. Modern life is just too stressful to handle without the assistance of something with which to mood-alter.

It makes sense that addictions would be a major barrier to self-care for women. We feel our one-down status in relation to men; our self-esteem tends to be shakier and more subject to the approval or disapproval of others. We are overworked, underappreciated, time-stretched, multi-tasking women. Who can blame us if we duck out of the sweat lodge for an ice cream or a trip to the mall or a nip at the bottle? No one, of course.

The only problem is that, over time, you're not ducking out of the sweat lodge occasionally—you're doing it almost daily. Your best friend (food, shopping, pills, wine, cigarettes, the latest boyfriend) soon becomes your master. Not only are you not taking care of yourself—you're destroying yourself. You end up ducking out all the time—missing your life completely.

Anne Wilson Schaef may be right that we're all addicted to something. Pema Chödrön agrees with her—she says that everyone is an addict, and what we're addicted to is avoiding ourselves. We are addicted to escape. We are too sensitive for this world, it seems, so we reach for something—anything—to help us make it through the day (or night).

Even if you don't think you're an addict, you can be sure that you have addicts in your life. You may not know it—even *the addict* may not know it. Addicts are notoriously secretive and good at fooling people, including themselves. But addiction is everywhere in our society and we're all affected.

• Begin by Just Noticing •

PAY ATTENTION to the various kinds of addictions that people indulge in—overeating, overspending, compulsive busyness, smoking, drinking, destructive relationships, compulsive working, negative thinking, gambling, sex and romance, prescription pills, and above all, addiction to perfection.

You don't need to do anything right now, just notice what's going on around you. And notice what's going on *within* you.

CHAPTER 7

SOME OF US SUFFER FROM DEPRESSION. IT'S HARD TO TAKE GOOD CARE OF YOURSELF WHEN YOU FEEL LIKE SH★T.

Depression is not sobbing and crying and giving vent;
it is plain and simple reduction of feeling. . . .
People who keep stiff upper lips find
that it's damn hard to smile.

—Judith Guest, novelist

APPROXIMATELY 12 MILLION women in the United States experience clinical depression each year, reports the National Institute of Mental Health. That's about 30 percent of us. About one in every eight women can expect to develop clinical depression during her lifetime.* I don't know about you, but just reading those statistics makes me feel depressed.

Why are so many women depressed? The people who study such things have some answers for us—some surprising, some not so much. First, there are biological factors,

★ National Institute of Mental Health. Unpublished Epidemiological Catchment Area Analyses, 1999.

like hormonal changes and reproductive, genetic, and biological issues involving PMS, childbirth, menopause, and infertility, which can contribute to depression in certain women. Second, there are social factors, like job stress, family responsibilities, sexual abuse, poverty, and the roles and expectations of women, which can also set the stage for depression for some.*

According to a 1996 report, "American Attitudes about Clinical Depression and Its Treatment," by the National Institute of Mental Health, major depression affects twice as many women as men. This is true across the board, regardless of race or economic status. Forty-one percent of women who reported being depressed said that they were too embarrassed or ashamed to seek help, while 50 percent cited denial as a major barrier to treatment.

This same study reports that the identical two-to-one ratio has been reported in ten other countries! I know that misery loves company, but this is the kind of company all of us should find alarming.

What's an even more fascinating statistic found in the report is the large number of women who think depression is "normal." More than half the women surveyed believe that depression is a normal part of menopause, and it therefore doesn't require treatment. More than half also believe that depression is a normal part of aging and that it's normal for

---

* National Institute of Mental Health. *Depression: What Every Woman Should Know.* NIH Publication No. 00-4779, August 2000.

a mom to feel depressed for a couple of weeks after giving birth. These women seem to be accepting depression as part and parcel of what it means to be a woman—they accept it rather matter-of-factly. As a result, less than half of depressed women will seek professional treatment.

These findings support the cultural trends we discussed in an earlier chapter—it seems almost universally accepted that women's lot in life is hard. So that when women experience depression, many just consider it "normal."

I recently asked a therapist friend of mine, Sam Beasley, about these statistics about women's depression and their reluctance to seek treatment, and he pointed out that women, in general, are much more self-conscious than men. Women are often reluctant to draw attention to themselves, particularly in a negative way. They don't want to be perceived as complaining or whining.

Among depressed women who do not seek treatment, many are probably self-medicating with food (or perhaps shopping, drinking, smoking, or some other mood-altering substance or activity). Research published in 1996 in the *Journal of Social Psychology* showed a strong relationship between eating disorders (bulimia and anorexia nervosa) and depression in women.* Experts in the field of addiction point out that eating and shopping are both misguided attempts at self-nurturing and that both forms of addiction

---

* Stattler, Willcox M., DN: "The Relationship Between Disorders and Depression," *The Journal of Social Psychology* 136 (1996): 269.

(compulsive eating and compulsive shopping) are pandemic among American women. When we're depressed, we head to the mall for a little "retail therapy" or to the nearby 7-Eleven for a date with Ben and Jerry. Millions of women are self-medicating rather than seeking professional help.

What are the reasons for women's depression? Undoubtedly they are myriad. Some point the finger of blame at men, at the medical establishment, at the advertising industry, at evil corporations and brutal bosses, at the high divorce rate, at a decline in traditional "family values," at the sexual revolution, at feminism, at the media, and more. There is plenty of blame to go around.

But for our purposes, does it really matter? I'm not interested in blame—I'm interested in solutions.

"Understanding is the booby prize," said personal transformation guru Warner Erhard. We understand that 30 percent of women are depressed—but understanding doesn't solve the problem. Action solves the problem. Here are my three favorite *A*'s: Action Alleviates Anxiety.

If we spend any more time focusing on women's depression, I'll end up in bed for the rest of the afternoon and so will you. And that won't get us anywhere on our journey to loving self-care. So rather than get depressed about women being depressed, keep turning the pages of this book and get into the next section—the heart of the book—which is all about the Power of Positive Doing. Read it and reap.

• Begin by Just Noticing •

HOW OFTEN have you been seriously depressed? Are other women in your family depressed? How many of your girlfriends struggle with major depression?

In what ways are their depressions similar? In what ways are they different from one another? What insights can you gather from witnessing someone else's depression? Any lessons to learn?

Do you know women who have cured their depression? How did they do it? Have you learned anything about your own experience with depression from seeing how others overcame theirs?

If a depressed woman asked you for advice, what would you tell her? If you got depressed, would you take your own advice?

Section II

HOW?

HOW CAN WE CHANGE OUR HABITS OF SELF-CARE?

Steps to Take in Solving the Problem

Do something. If it works, do more of it.
If it doesn't, do something else.

—Franklin Delano Roosevelt,
32nd president of the United States

A FEW YEARS ago I adopted my first dog—a little pound puppy, just five months old, a darling blonde dog with a black tongue and an underbite that gives her the oddest face, so ugly she's cute. She was (and still is) a sweetie. Her name is Fannie.

One afternoon I was walking her in my neighborhood, when my neighbor Peter pulled up next to us in his car. We chatted a bit and he admired my new dog. "I've enrolled her in six weeks of dog training classes," I told him. I was committed to being a very responsible dog owner. Peter looked up at me from his car window and smiled. "Just remember," he said, "dogs respond best to training with love . . . just like people." With that he waved and drove away.

His gentle words have echoed in my mind many times since that day. I've told friends that story, and reminded myself of it when I'm out with the dog. I heeded his advice and trained my dog with love. I am firm and compassionate. I correct her with authority and kindness. Love means providing her with structure, discipline, consistency, and good boundaries. I reward her with attention, affection, belly rubs, and "atta girls"—not with food.

But the real wisdom in Peter's advice to me was *not* how to train my dog—it was how to train myself. Everything that applies to training an animal applies to training a human, too. Especially the love part.

This section of the book is designed to give you an opportunity to train *yourself* . . . with love. Learning to care for yourself is a process—not an event. The fifty-two short chapters in this section are to be read one at a time, with some time and space in between. The first few chapters provide several basic assumptions and foundational ideas upon which the later chapters build, but if you're the kind of person who likes to skip around in books, then of course you are free to do so. It's your book, your process, and your life.

It is a truism that people who feel good about themselves take care of themselves. And the reverse is also true: People who take good care of themselves feel good about themselves. Which comes first? The self-care or the self-love? It doesn't matter. You can get there from both sides. And we're going to work from both sides in the coming weeks and months.

Your assignment is to read one chapter and work with it for as long as it takes you to get the lesson. This might mean one chapter a day, or every few days—or it might mean one chapter a week for fifty-two weeks. You are free to move at your own pace. Each chapter includes an experiment or exercise for you to try for a set period of time. At the end of a few days, or a week, you can decide if you like the results you're getting. Keep what works, and leave the rest. But be sure you give each one a real chance—don't abandon the experiments too soon.

There will be many times in the coming weeks that you will be uncomfortable with the process. That's fine. It doesn't mean anything's wrong. Change, even *tiny* change, can be very disconcerting or disorienting for a while. Be patient with the process, and with yourself.

Above all, do not consider this process just one more thing to add to your endless to-do list. Do not beat yourself up with *it*! Remember what my friend Peter said about the dog—"training with love." Make that your mantra for the coming weeks and months as you work through these chapters. Your goal is "training with love."

WEEK 1

FIRST, JUST NOTICE WHAT YOU DO AND WHAT YOU DON'T DO. DON'T TRY TO CHANGE ANYTHING— JUST NOTICE.

Whereas average individuals often have not
the slightest idea of what they are, of what they want,
of what their own opinions are, self-actualizing individuals
have superior awareness of their own impulses, desires,
opinions, and subjective reactions in general.

—Abraham Maslow, psychologist

SELF-AWARENESS IS THE critical first step toward understanding ourselves, and ultimately, to bringing about positive personal change. But watch out—that first step is a doozie!

Many people are so terrified to look inside that they keep themselves on a perpetual treadmill, always overbusy, distracting themselves in order to avoid the discomfort of self-reflection and self-awareness. It takes courage to slow down, stop, pay attention to your feelings, thoughts, opinions, actions, and habits.

My father is probably the least introspective, least self-aware person I've ever known. When I asked him about it, he replied, "Years ago when I was young, I looked inside and didn't like what I saw. So I never looked again." The result of not looking was a lifetime of being clueless—insensitive to what was going on with other people, oblivious to the subtleties of social interactions, and failing to see the impact he had on the people closest to him: his wife and kids.

The Greek philosopher Socrates stated, "The unexamined life is not worth living." The Oracle at Delphi said, "Know thyself." The French author Camus wrote, "An intellectual is someone whose mind watches itself. I am happy to be both halves, the watcher and the watched." Great thinkers, doctors, philosophers, and psychologists throughout history have emphasized the importance of self-awareness, being conscious of oneself. They all knew that in order to become the best we can be, we must first understand who we are now. If you hope to bring about any change in your behavior and habits, you must first know who you're dealing with. You do this by noticing—just noticing—your thoughts, words, actions, reactions, feelings, and moods. So for now, just notice. That is a lot to do, if you really do it.

• For This Week •

CARRY A small notebook with you to make notes about what you notice about yourself as you go through the hours and days. Watch yourself as if you were watching an alien from another planet—looking with new eyes at a creature you are trying to understand. Make note of behaviors, thoughts, feelings, actions, reactions, and conversations. When you notice these things, also notice any judgments that come up. Do you automatically criticize yourself for thinking, feeling, saying, or doing certain things? Do you get annoyed with yourself? What do you like about yourself? What do you dislike? And notice your thoughts and feelings concerning other people, too. Do you have a lot of judgments and opinions about others?

Remember, don't *do* anything right away about what you notice. There will be plenty of time for action. For now, simply be aware of it.

WEEK 2

PAY ATTENTION TO THE WORDS YOU USE—IN SELF-TALK AND IN CONVERSATIONS WITH OTHERS.

The inner speech, your thoughts, can cause you to be rich or poor, loved or unloved, happy or unhappy, attractive or unattractive, powerful or weak.

—Ralph Charell, author of *How to Make Things Go Your Way*

MANY YEARS AGO I made a horrible discovery. My father was living in my head—and he wasn't even paying rent! I had internalized all the critical things he said to me while I was growing up and they had become a central part of my mental self-talk. "You're too big to wear skirts like that" had become "You're fat." "Can't you do anything right?" had become "You're a screwup." "I'm not giving you any money for college—I'm not throwing good money after bad" had become "You're worthless" in my head. I didn't need Dad around to berate me anymore—I did a better job of it myself.

I know I'm not alone in this experience. In day-to-day

conversations as I listen to friends and others, I often hear their parents talking. I hear voices of worry, doubt, anxiety, hopelessness, worthlessness, despair, judgment, and criticism. Children learn the emotional language of the families they grow up in. Just as we learn English, Spanish, Japanese, or whatever language our parents speak, we also learn their emotional language. There is no way not to. Our minds are like little computers with blank hard drives. Our caretakers fill our hard drives with data, year after year, and this data is burned into our consciousness, much as one would burn data onto a CD. Then we spend the rest of our lives replaying the data, both in our self-talk and in our conversations with others.

The good news is that our mental hard drives are quite flexible. Experts call it "neuroplasticity"—a fancy word for "your brain can change, and so can you." It takes time and practice, but it's not as hard as you might think. It's simply a matter of learning a new language and using it on a daily basis. And the more you use it, the more it becomes second nature to you.

If you've ever learned a foreign language in school or at home, you can learn a new self-talk language, too. And like listening to foreign-language tapes to study, you'll have to use internal headphones to monitor your self-talk and start to change it. You can learn to catch your negative words and replace them with positive words.

The more you practice, the easier it will get.

• For This Week •

CONTINUE CARRYING a little notebook with you, and write down your negative self-talk when you hear it in your head, or in your conversations with others. Ask your friends to help you. Tell them that you're doing an experiment and you're trying to become more conscious of your language. They can't hear the words in your head, but they can hear the words you use in daily conversations. Ask them to interrupt you every time they hear you use negative language, so you can pause and write it down. You may find yourself filling up your little notebook very quickly. Don't be discouraged. You have to see the problem before you can solve it. And if the problem is bigger than you think, okay. You have your work cut out for you.

WEEK 3

GIVE UP THE STRUGGLE. MAKE PEACE WITH WHO YOU ARE TODAY.

It doesn't matter what we do until we accept ourselves. Once we accept ourselves, it doesn't matter what we do.

—Charly Heavenrich, naturalist

NOT TOO LONG ago I went to a conference hosted by one of my publishers. Upon arrival I noticed the office manager, Ginger Winters, had lost a lot of weight—sixty pounds—since the last time I'd seen her a year earlier. Ginger has always had a very pretty face, long shimmering blonde hair down to her waist, and a wonderful personality—but she had been significantly overweight for the fifteen years I'd known her.

"Wow, you look great, Ginger!" I exclaimed when I saw her. "What happened to you? How did you lose weight? You look amazing!"

Ginger's smile had a touch of irony. "Well, it was really

interesting," she replied. "After battling a weight problem my whole life, I finally decided to give up. 'That's it,' I told myself, 'you're going to be fat forever.' I threw out any clothes that were too small; I bought new underwear; I finally accepted myself just the way I was. Then the oddest thing happened—the weight just started to come off all by itself. I couldn't believe it! After giving up the fight, I started to lose weight without even trying."

"Fascinating, absolutely fascinating," I said. I, too, had struggled with my weight for many years, and it was a losing battle. I wondered if I could do what Ginger had done.

It sounds crazy, but before change can happen, *we have to make it okay not to change*. It's one of life's paradoxes—it is only by accepting ourselves just as we are that we create the conditions in which we can change.

You've probably heard that old saying, "That which you resist, persists." When you wrestle with trying to change something—in others or in yourself—you give it energy and power, thereby reinforcing the very thing you're trying to get rid of!

Habits, character flaws, personality quirks, attitudes—the more you try to change them, the worse they get. Anyone who has tried to lose weight and keep it off knows this all too well. The harder you try *not* to eat something, the more you want to eat it. Any wonder why diets don't work?

It was only when my friend Ginger gave up dieting that she began to lose weight. The other thing she told me was,

"Oh, and I dumped my husband. That helped, too." Ginger gave me a clue so many other overweight people have discovered: It's not what you're eating, it's what's eating you. We'll come back to weight problems several times in this book because overeating and eating the wrong foods are problems for millions of women. Turning to food is a misguided attempt at comfort and self-nurturing—a critical issue in any discussion of self-care.

• For This Week •

BEGIN THE process of accepting who you are today. It's not something you'll accomplish in a day or a week or a month. It can take quite a while for some of us. But by beginning to accept the parts of yourself that you've found unacceptable in the past, you begin to open up possibilities for change.

Pick just one thing you don't like about yourself and practice thinking of it in positive terms. Perhaps something like this would be a good start: "I *like* my thighs just the way they are. My legs are sturdy and strong and take me places I need to go. I'm grateful to my legs and thighs. Without them I wouldn't be able to walk. I'm so happy that they work for me. I like my thighs."

WEEK 4

DON'T LET WHAT YOU *CAN'T* DO STOP YOU FROM WHAT YOU *CAN* DO.

"Yes" is contagious on a subliminal level.
It affects everything you do.
—SARK, artist, author

MY FRIEND KAREN Cutts is a wise, loving woman. One day I was complaining to her about my problem sticking with my food plan, when she suggested, "Don't let what you can't do stop you from what you can do."

I asked her how that pertained to losing weight.

She explained: "Well, okay, you can't seem to give up sugar. Can you give up just one form of sugar?"

"Yes, I suppose I could give up ice cream," I replied.

"Great!" She smiled. "Then do that. You can't give up all sugar, but you can give up ice cream."

"Oh, I get it," I said. It made perfect sense—not just about eating, but about life.

"Don't let what you can't do stop you from what you can do" has become one of those simple guiding principles that helps me in so many of my daily activities. If I can't go biking because I live on a mountain, I *can* go hiking instead. If I can't play racquetball because I twist my ankles easily, I *can* go swimming instead. If I can't afford to hire an expensive personal trainer, I *can* afford an exercise DVD to use at home. If I can't go to an expensive spa, I *can* take a long, luxurious bubble bath.

Karen's words helped me give up my limited thinking, which had been a huge impediment to my own self-care. Now I do what I can, when I can, as often as I can. Just because I can't do everything doesn't mean I can't do *something*.

• For This Week •

PRACTICE THESE words as your mantra for the week: "I won't let what I can't do keep me from what I can do." Look for little things that you can do in areas that are important to your self-care. Maybe you can't go to the gym, but you can go for a walk. Maybe you can't go for a walk, but you can touch your toes ten times. It doesn't matter—just because you can't do everything doesn't mean you can't do something.

WEEK 5

CATCH YOURSELF DOING SOMETHING RIGHT (OR APPROXIMATELY RIGHT). THEN PAT YOURSELF ON THE BACK FOR IT.

Good women always think it is their fault. . . .
Bad women never take the blame for anything.
—Anita Brookner, English novelist, art historian

MY FRIEND KARYN has only one rule in her life: "I'm not allowed to beat myself up." She elaborates: "I got more than enough criticism and abuse when I was growing up. There were plenty of people beating me up, verbally and emotionally, if not physically. So now my only rule is—no matter what I do—I am not allowed to beat myself up."

Karyn told me how, years ago, she decided to go to the gym and start working out. She was overweight and self-conscious, but determined to do something about it. She got in her car, drove to the gym, and parked in the lot. Karyn walked from her car to the large picture window on the front of the gym, where she peered in at the svelte girls in their leggings, workout clothes, and yoga pants—then she turned around and went home. She just couldn't bring herself to go in. But instead of berating herself, she patted herself on the back. "Good girl," Karyn said to herself, "you went to the gym." She had honored her commitment to herself—at least she got to the front window.

Maybe next time she would manage to walk in the door. Perhaps she could work her way up to getting a locker. After that, maybe she could muster the courage to take a yoga class. And each step of the way, no matter how tiny that step was, Karyn would tell herself, "Good girl, you showed up. You did what you said you would do for yourself."

I can't tell you how many times Karyn's story has helped me. A tiny step toward self-care is still a step. I don't have to make giant leaps of progress—small steps will do just fine. And with each small step, I pat myself on the back.

If I am unable to take even a small step, that's okay, too. I still don't beat myself up. I know I am doing the best I can today, and maybe tomorrow a tiny step will be possible. But whatever happens, I am not allowed to beat myself up.

What would your life look like if you stopped beating yourself up? Neglecting our self-care doesn't call for self-criticism or recriminations. Goodness knows, we've all had enough of that to last a lifetime. Failing to take care of ourselves does not mean we have permission to use that failure as more cause for harsh judgments of ourselves.

Just the opposite. Failing to do what we know is good for us is a great opportunity to be compassionate and loving to ourselves, forgiving ourselves for our inability to exercise good self-care . . . for today. Tomorrow is a new day, and who knows? Perhaps tomorrow we will be able to do what we couldn't do today.

(In case you're wondering, today—some twenty years later—my friend Karyn is fit, trim, athletic, and a regular at the gym. She's in her fifties and has a body that many thirty-year-olds would envy!)

• For This Week •

CATCH YOURSELF doing something right. Any little thing—every little thing. Reach your right hand over your left shoulder and pat yourself on the back. Say, "Good girl. You just did something good." Because you did.

WEEK 6

SELF-CARE DOESN'T MEAN *SELFISH*.

The name of the game is taking care of yourself,
because you're going to live long enough to wish you had.
—Grace Mirabella, editor of *Vogue* magazine

ALL THE WORLD'S great spiritual traditions tell us to put others first, to be selfless, to serve others. We applaud self-sacrifice as a noble virtue, especially in women. Mother Teresa said, "Unless life is lived for others, it is not worthwhile." With similar messages from wise, respected sources all around us, it is all too easy to confuse self-care with being selfish. So we have some work to do here.

Whenever I feel concerned about putting my needs first, I remember what the flight attendants on airlines always say in their little preflight safety talk: "If we unexpectedly lose altitude, orange masks with oxygen tubes will automatically drop from the compartment above you. Please put on your own mask before trying to help your children or anyone else with their mask." I love this message. It means that I can't help anyone else unless I help myself first. If I try to put my child's mask on him first, I will pass out from lack of oxygen and I may die. Then I'm no use to my child or anyone else.

If I really love my children and want to be the best mom I can be, then I must take care of myself first. If I love my husband and want to be the best wife I can be, I must see to my own needs first. We women are the caretakers of the world, and in order to do this well, we must be caretakers of ourselves—first.

I must recharge my batteries first, so I can be a light to others. I must fill my own well first, so I can quench the thirst of others. I must feed myself first—physically, emotionally, spiritually—so I can then feed those that I love.

I am not being selfish—I am being wise.

• For This Week •

WHEN YOU find yourself concerned that you might be selfish, think of the airline attendant's instructions about putting on your own oxygen mask first. What do you need to do to give yourself "oxygen" today? Make time to do whatever that is. Maybe it's to take a ten-minute nap or find a quiet corner and meditate for a few minutes. Perhaps you need a snack of fresh fruit; maybe take a break and walk in the fresh air for a while. You're Number One—remember that.

WEEK 7

HELP IS NOT A FOUR-LETTER WORD. GET SUPPORT FROM OTHERS. NO ONE CAN DO IT FOR YOU, BUT YOU CAN'T DO IT ALONE.

Three of the most powerful words
in the English language are:
"Please help me."

—Cathy Conheim, therapist, author

THE GOOD NEWS is that women are much more likely to look for help than men are. More women than men go to seminars; women buy 80 percent of all books; women are more likely to seek therapy than men; and women go to the doctor more often than men. Women are less likely to get hung up on their egos and trying to figure everything out for themselves. All of this is good—we want to keep doing it.

The bad news is that some of us are still struggling with the Superwoman Syndrome—we think we should be able to do it all, all by ourselves. The Superwoman Syndrome is still alive, driving too many women to try to have it all and be it all—wife, mother, career woman, community volunteer, and all-around saint. We are more likely to try to tough it out when we get sick, thinking that we must rise from our sickbeds to take care of our families, and show up for work so we don't let the boss down. It's hard to ask for help if you think your job is to be Superwoman. It makes you feel weak, inadequate, and vulnerable.

Perhaps you were given the message that it's not okay to need help from others. Self-reliance is what most of us were taught growing up—"pulling yourself up by your own bootstraps" was considered the way of winners.

And what if someone says "no" to your request for help? It's a scary thought that your need for help might be ignored or rejected. But you'll never know how much help is available to you until you start asking.

Here are eight good steps to use when asking for help:

1. Be clear about what kind of help you're asking for. It's easier for others to say "yes" if they understand exactly what you need from them.
2. Pick the right time and place to ask. Timing is everything. Don't ask someone when they're in a rush, harried, or distracted. Wait until you have their attention and they're open and relaxed.
3. Pick the right person to ask. Some people can help you with financial advice, some with physical care, and some can provide emotional support. Think

about each person in your life and who you could ask for what kind of help.

4. Phrase your request in positive language: "Can you spare half an hour to help me with this problem?" (Don't put yourself down by asking in a negative fashion: "You wouldn't be willing to help me, would you?")
5. Don't ask for help, then micromanage your helper. He or she may not do things the way you would do them, and you need to be okay with that. People like to help, but on their terms. Accept what they give you graciously, even if you need to tweak things a bit after they're gone.
6. Don't ask for help and then reject or ignore it. That person will never help you again. Time is valuable and if someone takes the time to give you the help you ask for and then you don't use it, they will likely be resentful.
7. If the assistance you got wasn't as helpful as you had hoped, go back to the previous steps. Were you clear in what you asked for? Did you ask the right person? Did you get them at the right time and place? Don't blame your helper—look at what you might do differently next time to get help that's more on target. Show your appreciation. Be grateful in a sincere, authentic way. A warm, happy "Thank you so much for your help!" is always appreciated.

8. Offer help. What goes around, comes around. Watch for opportunities to help others.

• For This Week •

PRACTICE ASKING for help. If it's hard for you, start small. Ask for little things, like help carrying groceries to your car, or help understanding something that puzzles you. Ask different people for different kinds of help—your friends, your coworkers, your spouse and/or family members. Watch how people respond to your request for help. Most people will be pleased that you wanted their help. Not everyone, of course—a few people might be annoyed or too busy to help. Over time, practicing asking for help will show you who's available in your life—and what to ask of whom. You'll discover that there are plenty of folks who care about you and want to support you in whatever ways they can. You're in for some lovely surprises—and a little less stress!

LET GO OF PERFECTIONISM— IT'S BOTH A CAUSE AND A RESULT OF LOW SELF-ESTEEM.

Perfectionism is not a quest for the best.
It is a pursuit of the worst in ourselves,
the part that tells us that nothing we do will ever
be good enough—that we should try again.

—Julia Cameron, author of *The Artist's Way*

A FEW YEARS AGO I took a one-day class in furniture painting. Each student brought a small piece of furniture to paint. About halfway through the class, one of the women got very upset. She had brought a child's wooden chair to paint for her little niece and the chair wasn't looking very good. Close to tears, she asked the instructor what she could do to fix it—the instructor did her best to console and reassure the woman, but it didn't seem to help much. I watched the scene unfold and felt enormous empathy for the distressed chair painter. She so wanted her work to be perfect, yet, this being a class for beginners, that wasn't likely to happen.

Fortunately, I was in the midst of working through *The Artist's Way* with a group of friends. In the book, author Julia Cameron writes that you have to allow yourself to make bad art before you can make good art. Trying to be perfect is a surefire way to kill creativity. I knew she was right. "Bad art?" I said to myself. "I can do that! I can make bad art for sure!" And I gave myself permission to make bad art in the furniture painting class. I had a blast trying different techniques and all sorts of wacky colors and designs on the small coffee table I had brought to class. I decided this was going to be my sampler—just something to experiment with and learn from. If it turned out awful, I would try again on a different piece of furniture. I made a conscious choice *not* to paint perfectly. My table turned out great—*not* Picasso, for sure, but good enough for me to use in my home.

And the woman painting the child's chair? She was miserable for the rest of the day and left feeling dejected. Her perfectionism had ruined her day and destroyed any possibility of joy in learning by trying something new.

If you're a perfectionist, it's not a moment too soon to begin to let go of your impossibly high standards. Perfectionism will lead to chronic unhappiness because you'll never actually be perfect. Perfectionism will hold you back in self-care because you'll try to do that perfectly, too—leading to compulsive dieting and exercise, obsession with doing everything right, and tension from worrying that you're not good enough.

There is no quick fix for perfectionism. It takes a decision on your part to relax your standards, accept your human flaws and failings, and enjoy just being human—like the rest of us. Like a priceless diamond, whose unique flaws give it its character, you are perfectly imperfect. Give yourself permission—again and again, if need be—to do some things badly, to do other things with mediocrity, and to do a few things well. You'll find your self-care improves, along with your happiness with yourself.

• For This Week •

THINK OF something fun you'd like to try but don't know how to do. Perhaps it's a sport, an art, an activity, a job, a hobby—pick something you've long wished you could do. Acknowledge to yourself that beginners always do things badly—that is what it means to be a beginner. Give yourself permission to be bad at what you're about to try. Then go do it. Take that ski lesson, go snorkeling, sign up for a singing class, paint a canvas, write a poem, train for a new career—take the first steps toward doing something new, and doing it badly. Notice how you feel. Are you exhilarated? Scared? Excited? Eager? Nervous? Happy? Anxious? All of these things? Join the club. Everyone who is new at anything feels the same way. Feel your fear and do it anyway.

WEEK 9

FAKE IT 'TIL YOU MAKE IT. ACT AS IF YOU VALUE YOURSELF, EVEN WHEN YOU DON'T FEEL LIKE IT.

If you want a quality, act as if you already had it.

—William James, psychologist

Hamlet gave his mother some good advice: "Assume a virtue, if you have it not. . . . For use almost can change the stamp of nature." Translated into contemporary language: "Fake it 'til you make it." Hamlet understood what thoughtful observers of human nature have known for hundreds, if not thousands, of years. Human beings are capable of feeling one way while acting a different way, if they choose to.

Actors and other performers do this all the time. "The show must go on," they say, understanding that you must show up for your performance even if you're having a bad day, even if you're bored silly with doing the same show night after night, even if you just don't feel like it. Acting is being able to throw an internal switch and play your part convincingly, even if your heart isn't in it.

Those of us who are not actors can do the very same thing and it's quite helpful—especially when you're trying to develop a new habit, like a self-care habit. If we wait until we feel like it, we might never learn new behaviors and habits! So we must go to the gym, even if we're tired. We can choose salad from the menu, even if we'd rather have a pizza. We can say "no" to the saleswoman, even if we really want to say "yes." Acting in our own best interest often means "faking it 'til we make it."

Here's why it works. Psychologists have a fancy term for this behavior—cognitive dissonance. What we've learned about human nature is that a person's attitude and her behavior must be in sync for the person to feel at ease. When the person's attitude is one way, but she acts a different way, the result is tension or a sense of uneasiness. Something important is out of alignment and we feel it (dissonance) in our psyches and our bodies. One of two things will happen as a result: Either behavior will change to get into alignment with attitude, or attitude will change to get into alignment with behavior. That is why you can literally act your way into a new attitude! If you're consistent in your new behavior, your attitude *must* follow—sooner or later.

This is really good news for us in developing a new self-care lifestyle. If you keep faking it, you will definitely make it!

• For This Week •

PICK ONE self-care behavior that you'd like to become a habit. Write it down, perhaps as an affirmation. "I love going to the gym every other day." Or, "I choose healthy, fresh foods at every meal." Then *do* that behavior, even when you don't feel like it. Call a supportive friend if you need a little encouragement in the process. Join a support group so you won't be alone in learning to care for yourself. Make a commitment to "act as if" the new behavior is the most natural thing in the world to you. Soon it will be.

WEEK 10

WHAT WOULD RADICAL SELF-CARE LOOK LIKE FOR YOU RIGHT NOW?

If I'd known I was going to live this long,
I'd have taken better care of myself.
—Eubie Blake, composer, pianist

THIS IS ONE of my favorite tools: Throughout the day, I stop what I'm doing every so often and ask myself, "What would radical self-care look like for me right now?" I learned it from my friend Beth, who had spent years in personal growth workshops and self-help groups. I admired the way she took care of herself.

One day I was talking to Beth on the phone and lamenting the fact that I just seemed to have a hard time doing the right thing when it came to food, exercise, sleep, and sometimes in other aspects of my life, too.

"What would radical self-care look like for BJ right now?" she asked me.

"Huh?" I replied. It was a huge question—an important one—a question I'd never thought to ask myself. Basic self-care was challenging enough—but *radical* self-care was a foreign concept entirely.

Beth repeated the question. "What would radical self-care look like for BJ right now?" Then she was silent.

Wow. I was stumped. I really had to take a few minutes to wrap my brain around this question.

"Take a nap. Now that would be radical," I finally replied. "I'm really fried. But I have so much to do—the house is filthy, my car needs washing, the laundry is piling up, and I have a book deadline looming."

"What does your intuition tell you?" she asked gently.

"My intuition—and my body—tell me I need a nap," I replied.

"Then do that," Beth said. "Use this simple question as you go through your day. Every once in a while, pause and ask yourself, "What would radical self-care look like for me right now?"

I love this question. When I remember to use it, my life is great. When I forget to use it, I sometimes slip in terms of my self-care.

• For This Week •

WRITE DOWN the question, "What would radical self-care look like for me right now?" Write it on Post-it

Notes—stick one on your bathroom mirror, one on the dashboard of your car, one on your refrigerator door, one on your wallet. Use this simple question to keep you focused on radical self-care.

WEEK 11

MAKE A GRATITUDE LIST AND BUILD FROM THERE. WHAT YOU FOCUS ON IS WHAT YOU'LL GET MORE OF.

They themselves are makers of themselves by virtue
of the thoughts which they choose and encourage; that mind is
the master-weaver, both of the inner garment of character
and the outer garment of circumstance, and that,
as they may have hitherto woven in ignorance and pain
they may now weave in enlightenment and happiness.

—James Allen, author of *As a Man Thinketh*

THE HUMAN MIND is a mismatch detector—it will always notice what's wrong before it notices what's right. This ability to grasp what's wrong instantly is an important survival mechanism, dating back to caveman days. If you come home to your cave at night and something is amiss, you are alerted to danger. If something isn't as it should be in your immediate environment, you're on guard to protect yourself. The brain instantly sees that something is wrong and propels us to take steps to fix it.

But this mismatch detector in our minds can also be problematic. Our minds want to focus on what's missing, what's wrong, what we don't want. How can we ever expect to make positive changes if our minds are constantly glued to the negative?

But don't take my word for it. Listen to what people talk about: the traffic is getting worse; politicians are awful; the real estate bubble is bursting; the economy is a wreck; our planet is in trouble; terrorism has us running scared; we never seem to have enough money; we want to lose weight but can't; our spouses or kids are giving us fits; we're getting older and it sucks; our bosses are jerks. The list is endless. Turn on the TV, pick up a newspaper, tune in to a talk radio show—it is a relentless stream of bad news. We beat the drum of "ain't it awful" whenever we get together.

Well, here's what I can tell you for sure: What you focus on is what you get more of. Your energy follows your attention. If you're focused on what's missing in your life, you'll just get more of the same.

When I first learned this, I had to give myself attitude adjustments every so often. Sometimes I did it by talking with a friend; other times I did it through prayer or meditation; occasionally I'd just grab my head with both hands and turn it from side to side, making creaking noises, to indicate that I was giving myself an attitude adjustment. You can do it however it works best for you.

Even my stern old father knows the importance of focus and attention. A few years ago I asked for his help with strengthening my financial situation. Dad is a banker (as are other members of my family), but I seem to be missing the "financial gene." Dad expressed his puzzlement—he just couldn't understand how an intelligent achiever like me could make such a mess of her money. "I've seen what you can do when you put your mind to something," he pointed out. "You can do almost anything—you're amazing. I'm sure you can do the same thing with your money, if only you will focus on it."

Dad was absolutely right. I just didn't like paying attention to money because I found writing books, leading seminars, and the creative parts of my business so much more fun. I ignored money and hoped that it would take care of itself. It didn't.

So I've learned that if I want more money, I must pay attention to money. I must focus on it, cultivate it, nurture it with my attention and energy. Today I pay a lot of attention to my money—and guess what? More of it keeps showing up!

The same is true for you. Focus on what you do want, not what you don't want. Pay attention to your conversations throughout the day—are you complaining about what's missing, or are you celebrating what's right with your life?

• For This Week •

MY FRIEND Sam Beasley taught me the power of active appreciation: Make a little time each day to notice the things around you that you like. If you like your home and the things in it, spend a few minutes morning and evening walking around your home, touching and appreciating the things you like. "Ooooh, quilt, I like this. Give me more of this." "Mmmm, nice clothes. Give me more of these." "Ahhh, fridge full of healthy food. Give me more of this." "Good reliable car. Give me more like this." "Great family. I want more of this."

The Universe is a giant "YES" machine. It will give you more of what you focus on and show gratitude for.

WEEK 12

CLEAR AWAY NEGATIVE EMOTIONS: WORRY, FEAR, ANXIETY, REGRET, PESSIMISM.

Most people are about as happy
as they make up their minds to be.
—Abraham Lincoln, 16th president of the United States

A PSYCHOLOGIST ONCE told me that all kids are raised with either guilt or shame. "What's the difference?" I asked him. I thought guilt and shame were synonymous.

He explained: "Guilt is when you are made to feel responsible for someone else's happiness. Like, 'How could you do this to your sister?' or 'How could you disappoint your mother?' Shame, on the other hand, is when you are made to feel defective—that there's something wrong with you that is irreparable. 'Can't you do anything right?' is an indictment of shame."

I was raised with shame. Perhaps you were raised with

guilt. Some kids get a double whammy—they're raised with both shame and guilt. But almost nobody gets raised without one or the other.

Whatever your situation—raised with shame or guilt—it's essential that you find ways to heal it. If you haven't done that yet, do that first, before you do anything else in this book.

• For This Week •

TAKE AN emotional inventory of yourself—a list of the negative emotions that haunt you: chronic fears, worries, regrets, anxieties. List as many as come to mind. This is the baggage that's weighing you down—it's the emotional garbage that you long ago stuffed away someplace in your psyche and it's sitting there rotting. You need to get rid of this stuff.

There are many ways to get rid of such baggage. You can discuss your lists with a therapist and get some guidance about how to process your feelings and let them go. You can seek out a spiritual guide—such as a priest or rabbi—to read your lists to and ask for help in healing your unresolved stuff from the past. You can join a twelve-step group (e.g., Codependents Anonymous, Al-Anon, or Adult Children of Alcoholics); they have very effective steps you can take to get rid of your old baggage.

Sometimes the best help comes from trusted friends—those who offer a listening ear and a compassionate heart.

Above all, do not seek out someone who will try to "fix" you, or someone who commiserates in seeing you as a victim. You want a sounding board and a witness to help you rid yourself of old baggage.

The point is, seek out some help with this. You may be a person who can heal her old baggage by herself, but most of us can't. We need the support and guidance of a spiritual or psychological person or the support of a group.

WEEK 13

DON'T "SHOULD" ON YOURSELF. DROP THE WORDS "SHOULD" AND "OUGHT" FROM YOUR VOCABULARY.

I have never seen a person grow or change
in a self-constructive meaningful way
when . . . motivated by guilt, shame, or self-hate.
—Herb Goldberg, therapist, author of *What Men Really Want*

WORDS HAVE POWER and energy. Some words energize and inspire—others trigger dread and resistance. "Should" and "ought" fall into the latter category. They are not helpful in your quest for radical self-care.

Think about it. How do you feel when you say, "I should take better care of myself" or "I really ought to clean out my closet"? Do you feel fired up, raring to go? Does it inspire you to action? Does it give you the results you want? No. If you're like most people, thinking or talking about the things you "should do" or "ought to do" fills you with feelings of dread, resistance, and an overwhelming desire to lie down and take a nap. Nobody responds well to "shoulds"—"shoulds" induce fatigue, guilt, and depression.

"Want," on the other hand, is a positive word—inducing desire, inspiring action, giving you energy. When you want something, you're motivated to go get it. You get your butt in gear and start moving. "I want to take good care of myself" gives me a positive feeling, a little energy. "I want to clean out my closet" comes from desire, not duty.

Once a year, I sit down and make three lists—of all the things I want to have, be, and do before I die. These lists give me pleasure—they give me positive goals to aim for. And I love goals. I love to achieve things, to cross things off my lists when I accomplish them. When I make my three lists, I am happy and eager to get to work. I may never complete all the things on my lists, but that's okay—it's creating a vision for my future; it's opening up possibilities; it's focusing me in the direction I want to be focused.

But I *never* make a list of the things I "should do." Such a list would make me depressed, and I would want to stay in bed all day. I would feel tired just reading such a list. Because "should" is a word that depletes energy and depresses my spirit. Nope, no "shoulds" for me, thankyouverymuch.

On the other hand, "want" is a word that makes me excited, eager, and happy. "Want" comes from my heart and I love following my heart. I want to take good care of myself; I want to pay off my mortgage within two years; I want to go to the gym three times a week; I want to eat more fruit and veggies; I want to have a home free from clutter; I want to drive a clean car; I want to ride my bike more often; I want to travel to Ireland; I want to be current on my bills each month; I want to meditate every day; I want to improve my posture; I want to make time to garden; I want to reach my income goal this year; I want to write and sell books that help millions of women; I want to hike with my dog each day; I want financial peace of mind. . . . I could go on and on. You won't find a single "should" on my lists—only "wants."

• For This Week •

JUST FOR this week, drop the words "should" and "ought" from your vocabulary. If you slip and accidentally say them, catch yourself immediately and replace them with the word "want." Be patient with yourself. You may have been "shoulding" on yourself for years—it may take some time to break the habit. But keep at it. See if "wanting" something feels better than "should" or "ought." See if it shifts your energy and attitude toward taking good care of yourself.

WEEK 14

GO TO BED HALF AN HOUR EARLIER. SELF-CARE BEGINS WITH THE BASICS.

Early to bed, early to rise,
work like hell, and advertise.
—Laurence J. Peter, Canadian writer

I COULDN'T RESIST including Laurence Peter's riff on the old Ben Franklin quote, "Early to bed, early to rise, makes a man healthy, wealthy, and wise." What both men are talking about, of course, are the basics. One is pointing out business basics; the other is referring to personal basics. Both will lead you to success and happiness.

That's the biggest part of self-care—basics. It's not about froufrou soaps, expensive massages, fancy cashmere robes, luxury cruises, or expensive anything. Superb self-care is as simple as taking a nap, soaking in a relaxing bath, getting enough sleep, eating an apple instead of a muffin, saying "no thanks" when you're overcommitted, and going to bed just a little earlier.

"Many women are starved for sleep," wrote Janice Billingsley in an article for *HealthDay News* in 2003. "Start with the stresses of work and family. Add household responsibilities and perhaps worry about an elderly parent. Then factor in the hormonal changes that come with being female, and it should come as no surprise [that] many women are shortchanged on sleep."

Dr. Suzanne Griffin, a Georgetown University psychiatrist specializing in sleep disorders, says that insufficient sleep leads to poor concentration, irritability and fatigue, which can mimic symptoms of other health problems.* Some women seek medical help, thinking they have attention deficit disorder or depression—when the real problem is simply not enough sleep.

"Everyone expects women to be caregivers, and this is making them lose precious sleep," says Dr. Joyce Walsleben, former director of the New York University School of Medicine Sleep Disorders Center. "Women's lack of sleep has become a societal crisis bordering on a national health epidemic."**

---

* Billingsley, Janice. "Many Women Are Starved for Sleep." *HealthDay News*. October 10, 2003.

** Ginty, Molly M. "Sleep Deprivation Threatens Women's Health." *Women's eNews*. March 28, 2005, http://www.womensenews.org/article.cfm/dyn/aid/2235/context/archive.

In other words, the six and a half hours sleep that most women get per night is not enough. We need the eight hours that doctors recommend for maximum health benefit. It's not just "beauty sleep" we're talking about here—it's sanity sleep!

• For This Week •

LOOK FOR small, simple things you can change in your daily routine to enhance your self-care. Sleep is a great place to start.

It sounds easy, but going to bed earlier may be harder than you anticipate. We are, after all, creatures of habit. If you're a TV fan, you have your favorite shows. It can be hard to turn them off early, or skip them entirely. Perhaps your evening activity is reading and you're reluctant to put down your book. Or maybe the evening is when you get to your domestic chores—laundry, cleaning, helping kids with homework, going to the grocery store or drugstore, etc. If you're a working mom, you essentially have two full-time jobs, making it well nigh impossible for you to go to bed earlier. Late night may be the only time you have to yourself, a little peace and quiet "me" time.

But before you rule it out, give it a try—that's all I'm suggesting. View it as an experiment. If you like the results you get from making this change, keep doing it. If it doesn't work for you, go back to your normal bedtime.

WEEK 15

LOOK FOR WOMEN WHO HAVE WHAT YOU WANT AND LEARN FROM THEM.

When the student is ready the teacher will appear.

—Ancient Buddhist proverb

MOST PEOPLE LEARN best by watching someone else do what it is they need to learn. We then imitate what the other person does, and by following in their footsteps, we learn to do what they do. This is how children learn and this is how we adults learn as well.

Think about the women you know. Which among them are really good at taking care of themselves? What is it that they do, and can you learn to do it, too? Are there famous women who are exemplary models of self-care? Our heroines can be powerful role models, even if they are women we've never met.

Oprah is a prime example. You may or may not be an Oprah fan, but either way there's much you can learn from her. She's a woman who has struggled with self-care, particularly when it comes to food and exercise. She hired a personal trainer and continues to work out each week, even though she admits she often doesn't want to. Oprah seeks out other women to learn from—like Suze Orman and her books about money. Oprah learns from men as well—Dr. Mehmet Oz, who educates Oprah's viewers about important women's health and medical issues. Oprah reads a lot—she's an eager learner, always looking for ways to do what she encourages her viewers to do—"live your best life now."

So what we can learn from Oprah? Seek out experts to teach you what you want to know; learn from men as well as women; read; ask questions; be willing to admit what you don't know but want to learn; and have an open mind.

Who are the women in your life you can learn from? Who are the famous women you can learn from? And who are the men you can learn from?

• For This Week •

YOUR JOB is to seek out self-care mentors. And we all need mentoring—successful people in all walks of life will tell you that they had teachers, role models, and mentors who taught them what they needed to do to be successful.

Make a list of at least three people you'd like to learn from. You can list more if you like. Then make a plan for how you can learn from them: call them up and ask questions, invite them to lunch to pick their brains, simply watch and learn from a distance, read their book or watch their TV show if they have one. Put on your learning hat this week and see what you discover.

WEEK 16

PRACTICE ESTEEM-ABLE ACTS.

People who feel good about themselves
produce great results;
and people who produce great results
feel good about themselves.

—Ken Blanchard, coauthor of *The One Minute Manager*

EARLY IN MY career I attended a seminar taught by Ken Blanchard, coauthor of the timeless business classic *The One Minute Manager.* Ken said something very important that day: "People who feel good about themselves produce great results; and people who produce great results feel good about themselves. I don't know how to teach someone to have good self-esteem, nor do I know anyone else who does. Self-esteem is an attitude—how do you change someone's attitude? I don't know. But producing results is a behavior—it's external, not internal. So I focus on teaching people how to produce great results. I trust the attitude will take care of itself—self-esteem will follow from good behaviors."

He's right. So in the area of self-care, focus on actions that make you feel good about yourself. Focus on esteem-able acts. There are literally thousands of esteem-able acts that will raise your self-esteem: keeping your promises, showing up on time, paying your bills on time, doing something thoughtful for someone else, being generous, forgiving someone a transgression, being patient with someone who frustrates you, being kind, washing your face, dressing in an attractive way, washing your car, cleaning out a closet, organizing your desk, fixing something in your home that's broken, weeding the garden, mowing the lawn, cleaning the bathroom, cleaning out the cat's litter box, picking up your dog's poop when you walk him . . . the list could go on for pages.

You have hundreds of opportunities each day to do esteem-able acts—thousands of opportunities in a week. You don't have to do everything—but do something.

• For This Week •

START SMALL. Take baby steps. Commit to doing one esteem-able act today. Tomorrow make it two. The next day make it three. Keep going like that. Self-care habits are built slowly, over time, one esteem-able act at a time.

WEEK 17

LIGHTEN UP AND LAUGH . . . . A LOT.

Angels can fly 'cause they take themselves lightly.

—G. K. Chesterton, writer

SELF-CARE ISN'T SOMETHING big, complicated, or expensive. In fact, it's quite the opposite. It can be simple, small, and free—like laughter. Wise people from all walks of life know this. Swiss theologian Karl Barth wrote, "Laughter is the closest thing to the grace of God." Danish pianist and comic Victor Borge said, "Laughter is the shortest distance between two people." Playwright Henry Eliot wrote, "If it's sanity you're after, there is no recipe like laughter." American poet and philosopher Ralph Waldo Emerson wrote, "To laugh often and love much . . . this is to have succeeded." Humorist Arnold Glasgow wrote, "Laughter is a tranquilizer with no side effects." Actress

Katharine Hepburn said, "Life can be wildly tragic at times, and I've had my share. But whatever happens to you, you have to keep a slightly comic attitude. In the final analysis, you have got not to forget to laugh."

Norman Cousins wrote an entire book, *Anatomy of an Illness*, about how he healed himself from chronic illness with laughter: "What was significant about the laughter . . . was not just the fact that it provides internal exercise for a person . . . a form of jogging for the innards, but that it creates a mood in which the other positive emotions can be put to work, too." Cousins watched Marx Brothers movies, among other things, to induce healing laughter.

Want a simple, effective way to enhance your self-care? Laugh—loud and often. You'll feel better, get healthier, and live longer. For as author Ann Spangler wrote, "She who laughs last, lasts."

• For This Week •

THINK OF people you know who make you laugh. Spend some time with them. Rent funny movies and watch them, alone or with friends. Watch comedies on TV. Go to a dog park and watch the dogs having fun—dogs are often very funny. Read joke books. When you find an especially funny joke, call up a friend and share the laugh with him or her. Make it a point to laugh at least three times a day. See how you feel at the end of the week.

WEEK 18

GO ON A MEDIA FAST. BE VERY CAREFUL WHAT YOU PUT IN YOUR HEAD.

The newspapers! Sir, they are the most villainous, licentious, abominable, infernal—Not that I ever read them! No, I make it a rule never to look into a newspaper.

—Richard Sheridan, *The Critic*, Act I, Scene 2

A FEW YEARS ago I took an eight-week Artist's Way class on enhancing creativity. One of the weekly assignments was to go on a media fast for a week—no newspapers, radio, TV, magazines, Internet blogs, Web sites, movies, or any other form of media. At first I thought it was a silly assignment. "What does reading a newspaper or watching TV have to do with my creativity?" I grumbled to no one in particular. But I trusted the Artist's Way process, so I did as I was told.

As the days rolled by, I noticed how much I missed the media. It felt a bit like I was going through some kind of withdrawal—but it was a withdrawal from bad news, I realized. I went to museums; I walked in the park; I wrote in my journal; I worked on my creative projects; and I stayed away from the media. It felt odd, and I felt I might be missing out on whatever was happening in the world. Yet I discovered that if anything important happened, someone would tell me. By the end of our weeklong media fast, I felt very relaxed and peaceful.

The following week, I picked up my morning paper and started to read it. Instantly I noticed that something changed in my body—it felt like a bit of a downer the moment I started to read the front page. It wasn't a big downer, but it was enough of a negative shift that I could feel it. My week with no media had cleared my psyche of all bad news, and now I found myself hypersensitive to the newspaper.

After all, "news" is, by definition, that which deviates from the norm. If everything in the world is fine, that's not news. The only stuff that's news is negative stuff—fires, murders, crimes, assaults, bankruptcies, scandals, accusations, political chicanery, riots, wars, and bloodshed of any kind. Good news isn't news—so it never gets media attention. So it's no wonder the newspaper brings me down just a little.

In the years since taking that class, I still subscribe to two newspapers—the *Wall Street Journal* for business news (no blood there, just red ink) and the *Los Angeles Times*, my local paper. But most days, I don't read either of them. I may glance at the headlines to see if there's anything I need to pay attention to. More often, I save them 'til the end of the week, then spend an hour or two zooming through them, scanning for items that might be pertinent to my work, or human interest stuff that's sometimes enjoyable to read. Then I pile up the papers and take them to my local dog shelter, where they are used to line the bottoms of cages. So the papers don't go to waste . . . uh, well, they go to handle dog waste.

Think about what you put in your mind every day. How much bad news do you take in? What do you suppose it's doing to your frame of mind, your mood, your attitude, your energy level? Is this good self-care?

• For This Week •

GO ON a media fast this week. Just like we did in our Artist's Way class, you can see how the media affects your mood, your attitude, your energy.

If you have a spouse and/or kids, ask them to join you in the media fast—just for a week. Make it an adventure for the entire family. Explore new ways of being together that don't involve electronic gadgets or home entertainment centers. If they refuse to join you in your media fast, then ask them to at least support you in yours, and not watch TV or listen to the radio in your presence.

Unplug the TV (put it in the garage to be safe); unplug

your radio and put it in the closet; tell your newspaper company that you're going on vacation for a week and ask them to stop delivery; if any magazines arrive in the mail, stash them away someplace to read later. Unplug from any and all media. Instead of TV or newspapers, talk with your family or share a meal with a friend. Write a poem, make a collage, soak in a hot tub, sleep, go for a long walk, call someone you haven't talked to in a while—fill your time with activities that nurture your soul, your body, your friendships, your family.

WEEK 19

STOP PLAYING THE COMPARISON GAME.

When you are content to be simply
yourself and don't compare or compete,
everybody will respect you.

—Lao-Tzu, Chinese philosopher,
author of *Tao Te Ching*

HOW HARD IT is to stop comparing ourselves to others! From early childhood, we are always aware of how we measure up. Humans seem to be, by nature, keenly interested in our social standing relative to others. It's a trait and habit that sometimes helps us excel, but more often than not, it makes us miserable. As Max Ehrmann wrote, "If you compare yourself with others, you may become vain and bitter, for always there will be greater and lesser persons than yourself."

When I was in graduate school, I was a great student, earning top grades. There was another great student, too—his name was Paul. I always loved it when Paul and I signed up for the same class because being around him motivated me to work harder and do my best. It was like that old saying about the value of playing tennis with someone who's better than you, because it will make you a better player. That's how I felt about Paul—we enjoyed a healthy competition that made us both achieve more.

But I can think of many more times when comparing myself to others made me feel terrible about myself. This is especially true when it comes to body image. I have spent most of my life feeling that I was too fat or too tall, that my breasts were too small (as a teen) or too big (as an adult), that my hair was too straight, too thin, or too fine. Comparing our bodies is something that women do relentlessly, and the result is that many of us feel just awful about how we look. I don't know a single woman who feels great about her body!

And it's not because they don't look great—it's because they *think* they don't look great. It's a perception problem—not a body problem. Millions of girls and women today have "fat heads"—no matter how fit, trim, slender, and great these females look, their heads tell them "you're fat."

Learning to stop playing the comparison game is a lifelong challenge. It isn't easy, but it is essential to our happiness and health. We want to focus on our own well-being and ignore what others around us are doing or how they look.

• For This Week •

GREAT ATHLETES focus not on what other athletes do, but on something they call their "personal best." Each athlete knows what her best performance has been to date, and she has a sense of how much better she wants to become in her sport. She isn't competing so much with others as she is with her own best performance so far. She wants to top that. Essentially, she is competing with herself, not with anyone else.

Adopt this concept of "personal best" and use it in your own life. This week, focus on some aspect of personal care you'd like to improve—how often you go for a walk, how often you meditate, how many helping of veggies you eat, how often you take the stairs instead of the elevator, or whatever kind of self-care is important to you. Acknowledge how well you've done so far. What's your best benchmark? And make a commitment this week to try to top that. Walk one extra mile; make time for one extra nap; make a healthy breakfast one more day; say "no" to recreational shopping when your girlfriend invites you; do whatever personal care issue would be most beneficial at this moment.

It doesn't matter what your friends or anyone else is doing about their self-care—the only thing that counts is, what are *you* doing about yours? Focus on your personal best. You want to become a champion in self-care!

WEEK 20

DRAW ON SPIRITUAL RESOURCES TO ASSIST YOU.

I'm fulfilled in what I do . . . I never thought
that a lot of money or fine clothes—
the finer things in life—would make you happy.
My concept of happiness is to be filled
in a spiritual sense.

—Coretta Scott King, civil rights activist

WE HAVE MANY resources to draw upon in strengthening our self-care practices. Chief among these are spiritual resources: churches, spiritual teachers, synagogues, temples, ashrams, retreat centers, books, CDs and DVDs of our favorite spiritual guides and gurus. The popularity of people like Louise Hay, Deepak Chopra, Marianne Williamson, Wayne Dyer, Jack Canfield, Michael Beckwith, Esther and Jerry Hicks, and, of course, Sondra Byrne and *The Secret* make it clear that we are spiritually hungry people. We're fortunate to live in this day and age—never before have spiritual resources been so abundant and so widely accepted by people from all walks of life, and almost all faiths. There is a virtual spiritual buffet available—in bookstores, on the Internet, in spiritual settings—just waiting for you to pick and choose what you need to help you with yourself.

Nourishing and nurturing your soul is central to closing the gap between what you know about self-care and what you do about it. Spiritual solutions to our problems are the most powerful solutions we can seek. Spiritual answers provide serenity, security, and certainty in a way that no other self-care resources can. If you're committed to learning to love and care for yourself in deep, lasting ways, tapping into spiritual resources is the way to go.

• For This Week •

EXPLORE SPIRITUAL resources—teachers, books, retreats, workshops, CDs and DVDs, churches, temples, synagogues. Look to your own faith tradition first, of course. But also keep an open mind about spiritual paths that are new and unfamiliar to you. Buddha taught that we must adopt the "beginner's mind" if we seek to learn new things, for if we think we already know all the answers, there is no room in our minds to learn anything new. Practice having a "beginner's mind" this week.

ADOPT A FLEXIBLE NOTION OF SELF-CARE; ALLOW IT TO CHANGE OVER TIME.

Achievement of your happiness is the only moral purpose of your life, and that happiness, not pain or mindless self-indulgence, is the proof of your moral integrity, since it is the proof and the result of your loyalty to the achievement of your values.

—Ayn Rand, Russian-born American writer

DIFFERENT WOMEN HAVE different notions about what constitutes "healthy self-care." For me, having a cleaning lady come twice a month is a basic element of my self-care; for someone else that might be perceived as a luxury. For you, massages might be an important part of your regular regimen; for others, curling up with a good book is more important. It's up to you to define what constitutes good self-care—for you, not for anybody else.

Be prepared for your thoughts about this to change over time, particularly as you work your way through this book. What may seem like a luxury today might become a necessity to you in the future. As your level of awareness increases and your habits start to change, you may find that your priorities will change. How you spend your time, energy, and money will shift accordingly.

Nothing is set in concrete here. Start where your are today. All that's important is that you start.

• For This Week •

JOT DOWN three to five things that you think are essential to your self-care (whether you're currently doing them or not). Tuck this little note away in your wallet or someplace where you can easily find it again.

Once a month or so, get out the little note and see if you still think those same three to five things are important. Is there something else you'd add to the list?

Is there something that you'd delete? See if your ideas about self-care change over time.

WEEK 22

ASK YOUR FRIENDS WHAT THEY LOVE ABOUT YOU.

To attract good fortune, spend a new coin on an old friend, share an old pleasure with a new friend, and lift up the heart of a true friend by writing his name on the wings of a dragon.

—Chinese proverb

My friend David Wheatley called me a few months ago. "I'm playing a game," he told me. "Would you be willing to give me five compliments?"

"Of course," I replied. "But tell me more about this game. What are you going to do with the compliments?"

"I'm writing them all down and collecting them in a notebook," he said. "Then when I feel down or discouraged or bad about myself, I get out the notebook and read a bit."

"Does it work?" I asked.

"Yeah, it does," he answered. "And I'm having great fun collecting them, too. It's really interesting to find out how other people see me. I've had some surprising compliments, some funny ones, and some that seem sort of weird at first. I read them to my wife and we talk about them and laugh about them. It's turned into a fascinating game. Often, the compliment tells me more about the person giving it than it does about myself. So I learn about the people in my life, as well as about myself."

I gave David his five compliments:

1. I respect you.
2. I enjoy the interesting, intelligent things you have to say.
3. I like your approach to helping others.
4. I admire your happy marriage and thriving family.
5. You live a balanced life—I admire that.

Then I asked him to return the favor. Here's what he told me:

1. You have a strong personality.
2. You delight in things that go awry for their sheer humanity.
3. You're daring in your relationships; you're a risk-taker, a chance-taker.
4. You have this portable homebody quality that you take everywhere you go.
5. You're amazed by the world around you, one step at a time. You have this kind of steadfast amazement.

I loved it. It was fun, interesting, a teeny bit surprising, and it gave me insight into how David thinks, as well as how he sees me.

It made me think: We are all so quick to criticize one another, and ourselves. Wouldn't it be great if we took the time to compliment one another, to acknowledge what we admire in others, to tell our loved ones why we love them?

• For This Week •

PLAY YOUR own version of David's game this week. Ask your friends for compliments, or ask them why they love you. If you feel comfortable, ask your family members, too. (Though sometimes family members don't want to get into such intimate conversations—which may tell you something about your family.) Have fun playing the game. Keep notes on what people say.

Caution: Think carefully about who you play this game with—try to choose only those who will tell you *the truth with love.*

WEEK 23

PRACTICE USING AFFIRMATIONS TO RETRAIN YOUR THINKING AND YOUR ATTITUDE.

The more man meditates upon good thoughts,
the better will be his world and the world at large.

—Confucius, Chinese philosopher

I'VE KNOWN FOR a long time that I could change my internal dialogue—and in so doing, change my daily experiences, my career, my health, my happiness, my financial situation, my love life, and just about every other aspect of my life. That doesn't mean that I always do it—sometimes I forget, or sometimes I get caught up in negative thinking because I'm tired or ill or just running low on energy and enthusiasm. I'm an imperfect human being, just like you, and sometimes I forget to use the great tools I teach others. But sooner or later I remember, or a loving friend reminds me, and I'm back on track, harnessing the power of my mind and my words.

A few years ago I read Chellie Campbell's book *The Wealthy Spirit*. Chellie is a big believer in affirmations and they're an important part of the work she does in helping people with financial stress reduction. I've always been a big believer in the power of our attitude and expectations, but I had pooh-poohed affirmations as being a little too woo-woo for my taste. (I live in California, the granola state, but we're not all fruits, nuts, and flakes out here.) But I was experiencing financial stress and I committed to do whatever it took to turn my finances around. So I held my nose and did the affirmations.

The very first day I used the very first affirmation—"People love to give me money." I repeated it to myself as I walked my dog in the morning; I repeated it while I took a bath later in the day; and I repeated it as I drove to a restaurant to meet a date from the Internet dating site I was using. "People love to give me money" was my mantra for the day.

My date was lovely—he bought me a prime rib dinner, complete with wine and dessert. As we concluded our date, we walked toward the exit and he stopped at the maitre d's podium to get some change. He got his change, then turned to me and pressed a wad of bills into my hand. "Here's for the valet parking," he said, giving me a peck on my cheek. I smiled to myself as my affirmation echoed in my mind, "People love to give me money."

I used that affirmation all week. My cousin came over and handed me $100.

"What's this for?" I asked her.

"I owe you some money from a couple years ago," she replied.

"No, you don't," I replied. "I would remember if you owed me money."

"Trust me," she said, "I owe you the money."

"Well, okay," I said happily, tucking the bills into my jeans pocket.

Ka-ching. "People love to give me money."

I drove to San Diego to visit my mom for my birthday. My stepdad greeted me at the door with some Xeroxed articles and a $50 bill. "What's this? Birthday money?" I asked.

"No, it's for the postage for all those jokes you send me every week."

"You don't have to pay me," I protested. "It's my pleasure to send the jokes."

"I want to pay for the postage," he insisted.

Ka-ching. "People love to give me money."

And so it went all that week. Money showing up from unexpected sources—royalty checks, refund of a double payment I had made in error on my FedEx account, and more. "People *do* love to give me money," I happily sang day after day.

That cured me of my disdain for affirmations, big-time.

So much for woo-woo stuff. I'm happy to woo-woo all the way to the bank.

• For This Week •

IF FINANCIAL self-care is a problem for you, buy Chellie's book *The Wealthy Spirit*. It's a 365-page book, and you only read one page per day. Do everything she tells you to do, especially those affirmations. Watch the power of your mind at work as money begins to flow in. Let go of worry and negative thoughts—replace them with positive beliefs and affirmations.

It takes time, of course. You probably can't replace a lifetime of negative thinking in just one week. But you can start where you are. Begin this week, and practice affirmations consistently. See if it doesn't immediately begin to shift your thoughts, your feelings, your energy and attitude.

WEEK 24

MAKE SELF-CARE INTO A GAME. MAKE IT FUN, ENGAGING, INTERESTING.

All life is an experiment.
The more experiments you make, the better.
—Ralph Waldo Emerson, poet, philospher

MY COUSIN MARILYN is super health-conscious. She has had a valve replacement in her heart, and her boyfriend has a history of heart trouble. As a result, they both eat a strict low-fat, or no-fat, diet. Doesn't sound like much fun, does it? No mayo, no egg yolks, no bacon, no "normal" salad dressings, absolutely nothing—ever—fried, no chocolate, no garlic cheese bread, no prime rib, no Girl Scout cookies . . . there are many "no-no's" on the list. I would be very sad if I could never eat any of those things again.

But my cousin doesn't seem to mind one bit. She loves to cook and try new recipes, and she makes a game out of seeing how many grams of fat she can remove from each recipe by making substitutions. Fat-free sour cream in place of the real thing, no-fat whipped cream instead of real cream, fat-free sauces for meat and veggies, low-fat salad dressings, and no-fat cookies. Instead of salt, she uses a wide variety of spices, making her meals interesting and tasty. Whenever I have dinner with her, she proudly announces how many grams of fat are in each portion of the items she's serving. A big grin accompanies her announcement—she's clearly pleased with herself.

I never cease to marvel at how much pleasure she takes from her fat-busting cooking game. She has found a way to have fun with something that most people would find onerous, depressing, and/or annoying.

I think one of the secrets of women who are really good at taking care of themselves is this: They actually enjoy it. They like eating healthy; they like to move their bodies in exercise; they feel good about resting, napping, meditating, and getting a good night's sleep. They enjoy saving money and like the feeling of having a robust savings account. They seem to have no trouble avoiding toxic people, at work and in their personal lives. These women just naturally seem to enjoy the process of self-care. And if they're not enjoying it, they're sure doing a great job of "faking it 'til they make it."

• For This Week •

PICK ONE self-care behavior that you want to cultivate—something you don't like to do very much. Get creative and see if you can figure out a way to turn it into a game. You can count grams of fat and use substitutions, like my cousin Marilyn. You can watch TV while you walk on the treadmill or ride an Exercycle at the gym (or at home if you have exercise equipment gathering dust like I do). I found that adopting a dog made walking a *lot* more fun—I take a different route every day, keeping things interesting. Searching out new, exotic fruits and vegetables at the local farmers' market adds an element of fun to healthy eating. See if you can find a couple of ways to turn self-care into something fun. If it's fun, you're more likely to keep it up.

WEEK 25

DO SOMETHING PHYSICAL TODAY. ANYTHING. GET YOUR BODY MOVING.

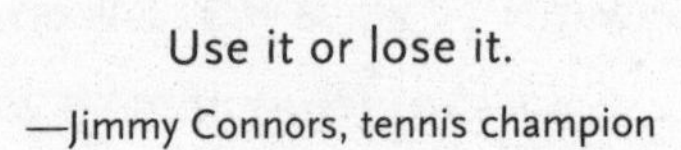

Use it or lose it.

—Jimmy Connors, tennis champion

I READ IN the newspaper the other week that new research reveals that thirty minutes of aerobic exercise every day can dramatically decrease your chances of developing Alzheimer's disease. A few weeks earlier, I tuned in to Oprah, who had Dr. Mehmet Oz as her guest for the day—he was citing studies demonstrating that regular exercise is more effective at curing depression than pills like Zanax, Zoloft, Prozac, and others. Every time I turn around these days, I'm hearing more and more about the curative, restorative, and preventive benefits of daily exercise. Is the Universe sending me a message?

Unfortunately, I doubt that walking from my desk to the

fridge and back counts as aerobic exercise. What the doctors and other experts are talking about is brisk walking, trooping up and down stairs frequently, hiking the neighborhood hills, or swimming, biking, jogging, or playing racquetball, tennis, or some other sport that will get my heart pumping.

Hmmm . . . I wonder if vigorous sex counts? I should check that out—might be a creative way to make exercise fun. Now, where is a handsome, hunky stud muffin when I need one?

Seriously, though, finding creative ways to get your body moving on a regular basis is a challenge for many women. Desk jobs encourage us to be sedentary; the convenience of cars keeps us from walking anywhere; and our too busy days seem stretched to the max already. Making time to move your body can be a real challenge.

One of the best things I ever did for my self-care was to adopt a dog from the local shelter. Fannie was just five months old, a mix of Chow and Pekingese, sweet, friendly, happy, and easygoing. I had never owned a dog before (I've always been a cat person), and I wanted to be a really good dog owner. I made a commitment to walking this dog twice a day, morning and evening, rain or shine, 365 days a year, no matter what. I thought this was the very least a good dog owner should do—and not just a piddling little walk, but a long walk at least once each day. Every morning we hike about two miles, up and down the hills where I live, and in the evening she gets a shorter sunset stroll of maybe a quarter or a half mile.

I've had my dog for six years now and I can count the times on one hand that I've missed walking her. What I discovered is that I am willing to do for her what I was rarely willing to do for myself. Before Fannie, I had a million and one reasons why I didn't go for a walk in the morning: It's too cold; it's too hot; I'm running late; I'm too busy; I don't feel like it; I'll do it tomorrow; ad infinitum. But making a commitment to someone else—in this case, my darling dog—gave me the motivation I needed to get my butt in gear every morning. ("Get my butt in gear"—that's a technical term I learned from personal-care professionals.) I often tell people that Fannie is my own little personal trainer. They laugh, but I don't care. Hey, I'm getting great exercise, meeting lots of people, enjoying quality time with my dog, and enjoying the fresh air every day—what's to laugh at?

• For This Week •

PICK ONE aerobic activity that you're willing to do for twenty or thirty minutes, three times this week. Trying to do it every day is probably too much the first week. But three times is definitely doable. Perhaps it's walking laps around the block at lunchtime, instead of sitting at your desk with your lunch. Maybe it's going swimming at your local YMCA. Or simply take your dog to a local park where you can run with him or her. Dogs make great exercise buddies!

WEEK 26

RESTING IS *NOT* "DOING NOTHING."

There is more refreshment and stimulation in a nap, even of the briefest, than in all the alcohol ever distilled.

—Ovid, ancient Roman poet

I BELIEVE IN practicing what I preach. Since I'm now halfway through the fifty-two chapters for part 2, I'm going to go take a nap. I'm *not* doing nothing—I'm resting up to finish writing this book. See you again in the next chapter.

• For This Week •

"THINK WHAT a better world it would be if we all, the whole world, had cookies and milk about three o'clock every afternoon and then lay down on our blankets for a nap," wrote Robert Fulghum in his lovely book about important lessons learned from kindergarten. So have a glass of milk—cookies optional—find your favorite blankey, and take a nap every day this week.

WEEK 27

FORGIVE PEOPLE WHO HAVE HURT YOU. FORGIVING THEM FREES *YOU*.

When you hold a resentment toward another, you are bound to that person or condition by an emotional link that is stronger than steel. Forgiveness is the only way to dissolve that link and get free.

—Catherine Ponder, author

At first glance, one might wonder what forgiveness has to do with self-care. But if you think about it a little further, I think you'll see the link. When we fail to forgive people who have hurt us, we are adding insult to injury. We are compounding the hurt by holding on to it, nursing our grudges, obsessing on our bruised feelings—all the while our hurt/disappointment/anger/resentment festers and grows like an emotional cancer. It kills friendships, families, marriages—it kills joy, happiness, peace of mind, and freedom. When we fail to forgive, we doom ourselves to a lifetime of slavery to our resentments, and we bind ourselves to the other person with negative energy.

Forgiveness isn't for the benefit of the person who hurt us—it's for our own benefit. According to pastor Lewis Smedes, "To forgive is to set a prisoner free and discover that the prisoner was you."

How can you take care of yourself if you're filled with rage at past injustices? How can you do what you know is good for you if you cling to all the hurts of your past? Unforgiven transgressions will pile up in your mind, in your heart, in your soul—like bags of uncollected garbage, rotting and stinking up the place.

This is especially true if the people you haven't forgiven are your parents. If you haven't gotten closure and peace with your parents, drop everything else you're doing and go do that. Because if you don't, I guarantee that the issues you have with your parents will continue to show up in your life in the form of issues with other people, other relationships, other situations. We carry these unresolved "parent issues" into our love lives, into our relationships with our bosses, and into more situations than most of us realize.

If we want to create a new future for ourselves, we need to clear out the "emotional garbage" to make room for new people, new experiences, new freedom, and new happiness.

• For This Week •

PICK ONE person you haven't forgiven for something that happened in the past. Find a way to forgive that person. Write him a letter or call her on the phone. Perhaps utter your forgiveness in the form of a prayer or make a peace offering to the person you need to forgive—a white rose, a beautiful feather, a polished stone—something simple.

WEEK 28

BALANCE YOUR CHECKBOOK.

Money isn't everything . . .
but it ranks right up there
with oxygen.

—Rita Davenport, humorist, author

"I BANK AT the fog bank," I often joke to my friends. They laugh—and I laugh with them—but it's not really funny. For years I've had a Scarlett O'Hara attitude toward money: "I can't think about that right now. . . . I'll think about that tomorrow." But tomorrow never comes.

The truth is, there are actually three things I don't like to think about: money (paying bills and balancing my checkbook), grocery shopping, and putting gas in my car. All three of these things are good for me—they're fundamental acts of self-care—but I don't like to do them. Why? Who knows? Who cares? Perhaps because I find them boring, not creative, not fun. It doesn't really matter "why"—what matters is what I do about them.

Financial self-care is a problem for millions of women. We like money (as do men), but many of us feel really incompetent at making it, managing it, or understanding how to make it work for us. Some of us were raised to think that money was dirty, bad, tacky, and/or shameful—"nice girls" don't talk about money, we were admonished. Some of us were taught that the way for a woman to deal with money was to find the right man, marry him, and then let him take care of the finances.

But sooner or later, many of us discovered that a man is not a financial plan! We can't count on marrying at all—much less on a husband who makes enough money to support a wife and family by himself. And some women who found such a guy later lost him to divorce—or widowhood—and the woman is left up the proverbial creek without a financial paddle. Yikes!

Germaine Greer, a pioneering feminist, wrote that a woman must have her own money if she is to be truly her own woman. Being responsible for your own life—creating your own future—means taking charge of your money.

Doing what we know is good for us means counting our money and making our money count. You have to know what you have before you can decide what to do with it—when and where to spend it, how much of it to save, how much to give away to help others. Financial self-care means leaving the fog bank and banking somewhere you can have clarity about your money.

• For This Week •

BALANCE YOUR checkbook. If it's been a long time since you've done so, you might need to reconcile three or four months' worth of bank statements. But don't overwhelm yourself. Start with just one bank statement—the most recent one.

If you live the "paperless life" and do all your banking electronically, you still need to review them each month—because banks do make errors. Go online and log on to your account. Notice the amounts paid and to whom, making sure that nothing is amiss.

If it seems like too much to handle on your own, ask a friend to sit down with you while you do it. You may not need help with the actual tallying—more likely you just need moral support. Make a pot of tea and ask a trusted friend (someone who won't criticize or laugh at you) to be with you while you tackle this onerous task. You don't need to do it alone. Ask for help if you need it.

WEEK 29

IT'S NOT WHAT YOU'RE EATING—IT'S WHAT'S EATING YOU.

Never eat more than you can lift.

—Miss Piggy, Muppet diva

NOWHERE IS THE gap between what we know and what we do bigger than with regard to what we eat. We know which foods are good for us—veggies, whole grains, fruit, olive oil, low-fat protein sources—but we don't eat them often enough. Instead, we find ourselves scarfing down fast food, caffeine, sweets, and comfort foods of all kinds. The gap between what we *know* is good to eat and what we *actually* eat is as big as the Grand Canyon—and getting bigger all the time (along with our waistlines).

I went to my local independent bookstore recently, checking out the books on women's self-help. One whole wall was covered with diet books—the Mediterranean

Diet, the Atkins Diet, the Beverly Hills Diet, the South Beach Diet, Dean Ornish's diet book, and hundreds more. No lack of information on how to lose weight, for sure.

But guess what was filling the wall facing all these diet books? Cookbooks—rows and rows of cookbooks! I stood in the middle of the aisle and laughed out loud. We are a nation obsessed with food—food we love to eat versus food we know we *should* eat. (Refer to what I wrote in chapter 13 about not "shoulding" on yourself.) We are getting fatter and fatter, while authors and publishers keep cranking out hundreds of books promising magic solutions. No wonder we're all confused and upset about what to do.

The core problem is that we're so focused on *what* we're eating that we completely overlook *why* we're eating. That's why diets don't work—98 percent of people who lose weight on a diet gain it all back (and more!) within two years. If weight is a problem for you, I guarantee you that a diet is not the answer.

Food is a mood-altering drug that millions of women use to deal with the stresses and strains of their everyday lives. Disappointing love affair? Ice cream will take away the pain. Need a jump start in the morning? A nice latte with a scone will wake you up with a jolt of caffeine and sugar. Boss driving you crazy at work? Nothing a candy bar or two can't fix. Stressed out by financial worries, family problems, career concerns? Comfort food is guaranteed to take the pain away for a while. Whether it's fried chicken and gravy, mashed potatoes, a pot pie, a grilled cheese sandwich, pie, cake, ice cream, cookies, Twinkies, Cheetos, potato chips, Cheez-Its, candy bars, brownies, mac and cheese, bread and butter, or all of the above, comfort food is what we turn to when the going gets tough.

Using food for comfort is not a uniquely American problem, nor exclusively a women's problem. Most cultures use food for emotional reasons: to celebrate special occasions, to express nurturing and caring, to console in times of grief and loss. Holidays call for special foods; family time involves eating together. Mothers and grandmothers throughout history have used food to say "I love you" to their kids and grandkids. Food and love are intertwined in millions of families around the world. Is it any wonder that food is the emotional balm we seek when we long for relief from our negative feelings? If emotional eating is a problem for you, know that you are not alone and that help is available.

• For This Week •

VISIT SEVERAL Overeaters Anonymous meetings. You can find them by looking in your phone book under "Overeaters Anonymous" or log on to the Internet and look them up. There are meetings in almost all cities and many towns in the United States. They also hold online meetings and phone meetings, if you can't get to an in-person meeting.

Many women know that they have a problem with food—overeating and bingeing, or bingeing and purging, or under-eating (anorexia—refusing to eat because they feel fat). All of these are simply different varieties in the general category of "problem with food." OA is a broad umbrella under which you can find help, no matter how distorted your relationship with food is.

Don't go to just one meeting—you need to check out several meetings to find out whether or not this support group is for you. Different meetings have different dynamics, different energy. Some meetings you'll like and others you'll dislike.

Emotional overeating may be only an occasional problem for you, in which case you may visit OA and find that it's not for you. That's fine. But check it out before rejecting it.

If it's not for you, at the very least you will have learned some things that may be helpful to recognizing—and avoiding—the dangers of emotional eating.

WEEK 30

GIVE UP THE NEED TO BE LIKED BY EVERYONE.

The telephone is a good way to talk to people without having to buy them a drink.

—Fran Lebowitz, humorist, essayist

MY FRIEND CHELLIE Campbell says that there are two kinds of people in the world: "your people" and "not your people." "Your people" are those who praise you, appreciate you, light up when they see you, and want to spend time with you. "Not your people" are those who ignore you, dismiss you, reject you, dislike you, and could care less what happens to you.

You can always tell who "your people" are because of how you feel when you're around them—you can feel the positive energy flow between you. You feel happy, comfortable, accepted, cared about. "Your people" are interested in what you have to say, what's on your mind, what's going on in your life. You always recognize "your people"—often as soon as you meet them. You feel like kindred spirits and you know you're among friends.

Chellie suggests that one way to have a happier life is to focus your attention on your people, and ignore those who are not your people. Your people will help you be more successful, support you in achieving your goals, and love and encourage you along the journey of life, no matter what. These are the people you want to spend time with—the ones who make a difference in your life.

How many of us get all caught up in worrying and obsessing about the people who don't like us—lying awake at night wondering how we can get their attention and perhaps win their acceptance? Does it ever work? No. If someone doesn't like you, there usually isn't much you can do to change their opinion—and why should you? But we women are so desperate to be liked, and deeply concerned that somewhere, somehow, someone out there in the world might not like us—and we drive ourselves crazy!

If it's important to you that everyone like you, then you're really going to be in deep yogurt when you start taking good care of yourself. When you say "no, thank you" to invitations you don't really want to accept, when you start making time for yourself, when you set healthy boundaries with people in your life, you can be sure that someone isn't going to like it—and someone may not like *you*. Gasp! Oh no, say it ain't so! Sorry . . . it's so. Practicing good self-care means that someone else may not like it, and may not like you for doing it. Get used to it.

Just recently I went through my online address book in my computer, deleting everyone who wasn't one of "my people." I was prompted to do this by a realization I had that I sometimes found myself trying to win someone's attention, approval, or friendship, when it was clear they really weren't interested in me. I was oddly attracted to people who were emotionally distant and unavailable—not just the men I dated, but also professional contacts and people I wished were my friends. Upon doing some journaling about this, I realized that I was re-creating the dynamic I had with my father—a man who was emotionally unavailable to me as his daughter. I discovered that I subconsciously gravitated to people, men and women, who were likewise emotionally distant and unavailable to me. Being around them felt familiar—just like home.

But I'm not a child anymore, and I don't need everyone's approval to feel okay about myself. And I certainly don't want to keep casting myself in the same role of eager, precocious little girl, hungry to be noticed and loved. Nope. No more. Plenty of people love me—*my* people love me and there are lots of them. Everyone else is *not* my people and it's time to let them go.

I felt enormous freedom as I deleted them, one by one, from my address book. I felt happier, lighter, more at peace with myself. I don't need the whole world to like me or love me—I just need *my* people.

• For This Week •

TAKE A sheet of paper and draw a line down the middle. On one side, list "*My* People," and on the other side, list "*Not* My People." Write down the names of all the people in your life—family, friends, coworkers, neighbors, and others. Sort them out in those two categories and see what you discover.

You may or may not choose to do anything about those who are "not your people"—it's totally up to you. No need to make any decisions about whether or not to keep them in your life. For now, just notice who "your people" are, and choose to spend more time with them. Let them love you, encourage you, support you, make you feel good. Self-care can be as simple as hanging out with "your people."

WEEK 31

NEVER PASS UP AN OPPORTUNITY TO PEE.

There are three kinds of men.
The one that learns by reading.
The few who learn by observation.
The rest of them have to pee
on the electric fence for themselves.
—Will Rogers, American humorist

IGNORING OUR FUNDAMENTAL biological needs is one of the worst ways women put themselves last. Some women are so accustomed to ignoring their own needs that they don't even take time to pee! "Oh, I can wait 'til I get home," they tell themselves as they're out running errands. Or, "I can hold it a little while longer," because they're in a hurry to do something else. Hunger, thirst, fatigue, and sleepiness—and the urge to pee—are important signals our bodies send us. We ignore them at our own peril.

In my opinion, it's the ultimate act of self-neglect. Did you know that you can get a painful bladder infection by holding your urine too long? It happens to thousands of women every year—women traveling on airplanes who don't like to use the onboard latrines, women in cars who don't want to take time to stop at a gas station's bathroom, and women just out and about in their daily lives.

Would you continue to drive your car if the gas gauge was on empty? Would you keep going anyway if the oil light lit up on your dashboard? Would you drive around on tires that were half-flat? "Maybe," you say, "if where I was going was important enough and I thought I could make it." But to do so is risky at best, and downright dangerous at worst. Why put yourself in harm's way like that? Because that's what we women do sometimes—we underestimate how serious something is until it's too late.

We take foolish risks, like the guys in the quote above, having to learn lessons the hard way, by peeing on the electric fence. What Will Rogers is telling us in his folksy way is that men often do dumb things, too—often learning their lessons the hard way. Small comfort, eh?

• For This Week •

DON'T PASS up an opportunity to pee. Just do it.

WEEK 32

ASK YOURSELF, "WHAT'S THE BEST USE OF MY TIME RIGHT NOW?"

Time is really the only capital that any human being has, and the only thing he can't afford to lose.

—Thomas Edison, scientist, inventor

HERE'S THE CENTRAL problem for today's busy woman: Each day she has ten things that need doing, but time enough to do only six. Her challenge is to pick the most important six things and do them, let go of the other four, and sleep peacefully at night, knowing she made the right choices.

The most effective time management tool I ever learned is this simple question: "What's the best use of my time right now?" I ask it of myself several times a day to stay focused on what's really important. It is so easy to get distracted or sidetracked by things that seem to need my attention, then eat up my time and energy, but ultimately aren't aligned with my goals and values. "What's the best use of my time right now?" helps me stay on target and on purpose.

I'll give you a few examples:

- If I'm attending a seminar that is boring, poorly presented, or has no helpful information, I'll ask myself, "What's the best use of my time right now?" If my answer is, "Not this seminar," then I discreetly slip out the back door and go do whatever it is that is more important and/or urgent.
- When I'm teaching a workshop or seminar, I even go so far as to tell my participants that they should use the same question: "What's the best use of my time right now?" If their time is better spent doing something other than attending a workshop of mine, I encourage them to excuse themselves at an appropriate time and go do something else. After all, the second-worst sin I can commit is to waste someone else's precious time. The worst sin is to waste my own!
- When I'm at a social gathering that isn't fun or interesting, I'll quietly say good night to the host and excuse myself with, "I have another commitment I must keep . . . but I'm glad I could at least stop by for a little while. Thank you for inviting me."

(The host doesn't need to know that the "other commitment" is to myself!)

- Whenever I find myself engaged in any activity that isn't congruent with my goals or values, I stop what I'm doing, then take steps to move in a direction more aligned with what's important to me.

To paraphrase Ben Franklin: If you love life—if you love *your* life—then don't waste time, not even an hour, not even a minute. For time is the stuff that life is made of.

• For This Week •

MAKE IT a point to ask yourself several times every day, "What's the best use of my time right now?" Pay attention to what your intuition tells you. Notice if your head tells you one thing (watch out for those "shoulds") but your intuition tells you something else. Trust your instincts. Choose those activities that are the best use of your time.

Don't worry about what other people will think. You might be pleasantly surprised to discover that they will actually respect you more for using your time wisely.

WEEK 33

CLEAN OUT ONE DRAWER OR ONE CLOSET.

When you break a big project into smaller chunks—
into tiny projects—you stand a better chance at maintaining
motivation and rekindling interest. When you have a pile of
tiny projects, you get the chance to work on something
new more often. We do our best work when we're
excited about starting something new.

—Jason Fried, 37signals.com

FOR MUCH OF my life I was an all-or-nothing person. If I couldn't clean my whole house, I wouldn't clean any of it. If I couldn't complete a project in the amount of time I had available, I wouldn't work on the project at all. In high school I would pull all-nighters to write my term papers in one sitting, adrenaline pumping through my body.

I'm not sure why I was this way. Perhaps it was simply inertia—once I got moving, my momentum made me want to just keep moving until I completed whatever I was doing. A body at rest tends to stay at rest and a body that's moving tends to keep moving—at least when the body is mine.

But this inertia principle of mine didn't serve me well. Things that needed doing just sat there until I had enough time to do the whole thing. I shudder to think how long stuff sat around, unattended, until I was ready to deal with it in one fell swoop. Those all-or-nothing days were not my most productive.

Then I learned about time management from a friend at work. I enrolled in a one-day seminar, where I learned some basic tools—not just how to manage time, but how to manage my life! One of the most helpful tools learned was "chunking"—breaking big projects down into smaller, doable chunks. It seems so simple, so obvious, so much common sense. But common sense isn't always so common. At least it wasn't with me.

With my new chunking method, I could wash the windows in one room of the house, if I only had an hour. The rest of the windows in the house could wait for another day. I could clean out one kitchen cabinet, even if I didn't have time to clean out all of them. I could reorganize one drawer in my desk, and do another one tomorrow. I could write one chapter in my next book, and come back another day to do the next chapter. I could call one friend just to say hi. In short, I learned how to chunk my household chores, my work projects, my life.

I'm reminded of that old joke: How do you eat an elephant? Answer: One bite at a time. I've learned that I can get a lot done in a day, in an hour, in fifteen minutes, if I take things one bite at a time.

All-or-nothing thinking—rest in peace.

• For This Week •

CLEAN OUT one drawer—or one closet—this week. Just one. Not all the drawers, not even two. Just do one. See how that feels. Next week you can do another one.

WEEK 34

MAKE APPOINTMENTS WITH YOURSELF.

I think you have to take charge of your own life and understand that you're either going to live somebody else's dream or live your own dream.

—Wilma Mankiller, Cherokee Nation first female chief

HOW OFTEN DO you make commitments to yourself, only to bail out on them when someone asks something of you? If you're like most women, you almost always show up for others, but you rarely show up for yourself. We are so conditioned to put others' needs above our own that it seems only natural to excuse our choices with, "My friend needed me; I didn't want to let her down," or, "I feel guilty if I say 'no,'" or, "I didn't want to hurt his feelings." After all, we rationalize, we can take care of our own needs later. Isn't it better to say "yes" to people who need us—even if it means saying "no" to ourselves? Isn't self-sacrifice a virtue after all?

We women have been saying "yes" to others and "no" to ourselves for millennia. Isn't it time we begin to change that?

One of the most empowering things I've learned to do over the years is to make appointments with myself. These aren't hair appointments or manicure appointments or doctor's appointments—though those are certainly worth making and keeping. These appointments with myself might be to watch *Oprah* and a few TV soaps for an afternoon, to take myself to a lovely al fresco lunch at my favorite café, or to do nothing—absolutely nothing—but putter around the house in my jammies. An appointment with myself is "me time." No questions asked, none answered. If something comes up and someone asks for that time, I look at my calendar and reply, "Oh, I already have an appointment at that time." I don't explain the appointment—I don't have to—it's nobody's business but mine.

Scheduling regular appointments with myself is a very simple, powerful way of putting myself first—where I belong.

• For This Week •

MAKE AN appointment with yourself this week. This appointment can be as simple as scheduling time to take a nap, go to an art museum, get a pedicure, or just do nothing. Treat these appointments just as you would any appointment for a business meeting or doctor's appointment. Write them on your calendar. If something comes up or someone asks for that time, simply say, "I'm sorry, I already have an appointment at that time. Can you suggest an alternative and I'll see if I'm available?"

WEEK 35

HONOR YOUR FEELINGS, BUT DON'T BE A SLAVE TO THEM.

You cannot make yourself feel something
you do not feel, but you can make yourself
do right in spite of your feelings.
—Pearl S. Buck, Nobel Prize–winning author

FEELINGS ARE LIKE the weather—they come and they go, sometimes quite unexpectedly, sometimes even violently. We do not try to change the weather, nor need we try to change our feelings. All we need to do is acknowledge them, notice them, and proceed with what we're committed to. We may have to accommodate a particularly strong feeling, much as we might accommodate a particularly strong storm—we might wait for it to die down a bit before we drive our cars in it. Likewise, we might want to do some journaling or call a friend if we're having a particularly tough time with emotions today.

Feelings and emotions are real and they can be powerful.

You're entitled to your feelings—they're legitimate and authentic, and no one else has the right to tell you how to feel. But just because feelings are real doesn't mean you need to act on them. If people acted on every feeling, the world would be chaos. We need only watch the evening news on TV to see what happens when people are unwilling or unable to handle their feelings constructively.

When you feel sad, it's normal to cry and express your sadness. When you're happy, it's appropriate to show that as well. If you feel disappointed, it's okay to acknowledge it. When angry, it's fine to feel angry. But everything within limits. It's healthy to notice our feelings, feel them to the fullest, express them in appropriate ways in the right time and place. Healthy maturity means being able to honor your feelings but not let them run your life, or act out inappropriately.

When two-year-olds feel angry, they throw tantrums. Mature adults don't. We feel our anger without lashing out to hurt someone else, or ourselves. When someone hurts us, we may want to punch his lights out, but we don't. We know better. Healthy self-care means paying attention to our feelings but not becoming slaves to them.

• For This Week •

PAY SPECIAL attention to your feelings this week. Treat your feelings like the weather. Notice how you feel when you first wake up in the morning. What's your emotional weather report? How do your feelings change throughout the day? You might want to jot down notes to yourself as your feelings shift and change. Feelings come and go all day long, all week long, all year long. Most of the time, there's nothing we need to do about them—just notice. Wait long enough, and like the weather, your feelings will change.

WEEK 36

DON'T GO TO A DRY WELL FOR WATER. SEEK OUT THE RIGHT PEOPLE TO SUPPORT YOU IN CARING FOR YOURSELF.

With true friends . . .
even water drunk together is sweet enough.
—Chinese proverb

It's disappointing to learn that some of the people in our lives are dry wells. It's even more painful to realize that those we want most to be there for us—family members such as spouses, parents, brothers, or sisters—may be unavailable for what we need. But it's important that we recognize the truth about these people so we can stop going to them for what they don't have to give. It's foolish to keep going back to a dry well for water.

I've had many years to heal the difficult relationship with my dad, and I'm happy to report that things are pretty good between us today. I've learned to accept him just the way he is, and just the way he isn't.

But occasionally I forget, when I want to share some especially exciting news about my career accomplishments. Last year I gave him a copy of my new business book, *YES Lives in the Land of NO*. I had worked very hard on the book and was thrilled with the final result—it was my best book in a number of years. I handed Dad the book and without even looking at it, he set it down on the coffee table and kept talking. The whole afternoon went by and he never said a word. Not "Hey, great, your new book!" or "This looks terrific, honey," not even a simple "Thank you." It was as if nothing had happened. And it hurt my feelings. Even after all these years of coming to understand his narcissism and self-absorption, it still stings just a little when he fails to acknowledge something I think is pretty important. It's a big deal to get a book published and most people know this—but not Dad.

So once again, I have to remind myself not to go to an empty well for water. If I want a pat on the back, I need to remember to go to people who love my books. When I'm hungry for an "atta girl," I need to go to my friends and fans—who appreciate me and my work.

• For This Week •

WHO ARE the dry wells in your life? Jot down the names of those people who are *not* available for support, acknowledgment, and encouragement. Read it over to yourself a few times.

Now, jot down the names of people in your life who *are* available to you. Read this list to yourself a few times. Then put the list in your wallet or tape it to your mirror or put it someplace where you can refer to it when you're in need of some cool, refreshing "water" of love and support.

WEEK 37

PUT YOUR CREDIT CARDS IN A JAR OF WATER AND FREEZE THEM.

Life was a lot simpler when
what we honored was father and mother,
rather than all major credit cards.
—Robert Orben, magician, comedy writer

ARE YOU A woman who shops too much? Are you worried about your debts? Do you buy things impulsively, on emotion? If so, you're not alone. Recreational shopping and impulse buying are common activities for millions of women. For we all know that when the going gets tough, the tough go shopping. "Retail therapy" it's called, or "mall therapy." It's the urge to comfort yourself with clothes, pretty things for your home, trinkets and baubles, nice things for your kids, gifts for others, and any other thing your creative brain can think of. Shopping triggers endorphins and other chemicals in the brain, making us feel better—for the time being. But the good feelings wear off and we're still left with the stress that made us go shopping in the first place, and often we are left with credit card debt as well, which only compounds our stress. We have to work harder and harder to keep up with our minimum monthly payments. We end up as slaves in servitude to King Mastercard and Queen Visa.

We know that shopping for things we don't need isn't good for us, but we do it anyway. We're facing another huge gap between what we know and what we do. Long-term self-care suffers at the expense of short-term quick fixes—which don't really fix anything.

The best way I know of to short-circuit the impulse to shop is to slow the shopper down, giving her enough time to think about what it is she is about to do. If she can pause long enough to reflect on what's really driving her to shop and what the shopping will or won't do for her, there is a chance she can turn away from the mall and turn toward something that might actually help her—like a phone call to a good friend, prayer or meditation, journaling about her feelings, or simply a nap.

Saying "no" to impulse shopping is a huge step in the direction of healthy self-care. Set yourself up to be successful by stashing your credit cards someplace where they won't be easy to get to.

• • •

• For This Week •

TAKE ALL your credit cards and put them in a jar of water. Then put the jar in your freezer. Be sure not to fasten the jar lid tightly—leave it loose because water expands as it freezes and you don't want the jar to break.

When you get the impulse to use your cards to go shopping, take ten minutes to think about why you want to buy something. Be honest with yourself. Is this urge to purchase driven by real needs, or by emotions and feelings? If at the end of ten minutes you still want to go shopping, you can unfreeze your cards and go, of course. The purpose of freezing the cards is not to prevent you from ever shopping again, but rather to help you be conscious of what's really driving your behavior, and to distinguish between "needs" and "wants."

WEEK 38

WASH A WINDOW OR TWO IN YOUR HOME OR APARTMENT.

I am thankful for a lawn that needs mowing,
windows that need cleaning, and gutters that need fixing
because it means I have a home. . . . I am thankful for
the piles of laundry and ironing because it means
my loved ones are nearby.

—Nancie J. Carmody, in *Family Circle* magazine, 1999

I LOVE A clean house—but I don't like to clean. I love sparkling windows—but I don't like to do them. I love a clean car—but I don't like to wash it. I love a tidy yard—but I don't like to trim hedges, rake leaves, or pull weeds. Obviously, I have a dilemma.

One way I can get all these clean, tidy, sparkling things I enjoy so much is to pay someone else to do them. And I do that. My cleaning lady is an important part of my self-care. She isn't a luxury—for me, she's a necessity. She comes every other Monday and those two days a month are my favorites. When she leaves, I feel refreshed, happy, energized, and optimistic. She makes my life so much easier—freeing me up to do the things that only I can do, like writing my books.

I feel the same way about the guys at the car wash who detail my car a couple times a year. I feel better about myself when I drive around in a clean, shiny car. It doesn't matter that the car is twenty-three years old—what matters is that it sparkles.

There have been times in my life, however, when I felt I couldn't afford to hire a cleaning lady or to take my car to the car wash. In those days I washed my own car and cleaned my own house. But I didn't do it all at once. Sometimes I would vacuum and dust just one room, the living room, because that's where I spent the most time. A couple days later I might clean the kitchen. A few days after that, I would scrub the bathroom.

Today, I still do that with my windows because my cleaning lady doesn't do windows. This week I will wash my living room windows because they are big picture windows, and most obviously dirty. That will take less than an hour and I know I will feel great when I'm done. Perhaps next week, I will wash the windows in my home office, so I can enjoy the view when I look up from my work. At the end of the month, I'll wash my bedroom windows—they are louvered and the dirt isn't as obvious as it is on other windows in the house.

Washing my own windows does several good things at once: I get a little exercise, especially in my upper arms where I need it most. I'll get instant gratification when I step back and admire my crystal clear view. I'll feel grateful that I have windows to wash. Every time I clean anything in my house, it feels as if I am appreciating my house—stroking, caressing, touching things that I find attractive. It makes me very happy. Even if I just dust the coffee table and do nothing else—or wash one window and do nothing else. Every little thing I am willing to do to clean and care for my home, and the things in it, makes me feel good about myself. I don't know if cleanliness really is next to godliness, but I do know that I feel virtuous after I wash a window. Every time I clean something, my halo shines a little brighter.

• For This Week •

WASH A window this week. Not all of them—just one. See how it makes you feel.

WEEK 39

WRITE DOWN EVERYTHING YOU SPEND THIS WEEK. YES, EVERY SINGLE PENNY.

Don't tell me where your priorities are.
Show me where you spend your money
and I'll tell you what they are.

—James W. Frick, educator

YOUR CHECKBOOK IS like a Rorschach inkblot test—it provides a fascinating glimpse into your psyche. If you want to get some insight into someone, just review his or her monthly checking account statements, along with his or her credit card statements, and you'll know an enormous amount about this person. You'll find out if the person has a family, whether or not there are health problems, how they spend their leisure time, what kind of food they eat, whether or not they are active or athletic, whether they're homebodies or travelers, and often you can even figure out their religion. How a person spends her money speaks volumes about how she thinks and feels.

Paying attention to how to spend your own money will help you understand yourself, and why you don't always do the things you know are good for you. Because self-esteem—or the lack of it—is often revealed in what we do with our dollars. Women (and men) who have low or erratic self-esteem will often buy things to make themselves feel better. Women will usually buy clothes and jewelry to make themselves feel prettier; they may also spend money on health clubs, plastic surgery, self-help books and seminars, as well as years of therapy. (Guys are more likely to buy gadgets and electronics, sporting goods, cars, and home entertainment systems to create a man-cave where they can feel like kings in their own castles. Money spent on porn and sexual experiences, as well as serious gambling, can also indicate self-esteem issues with men.)

Self-care begins with self-knowledge. You need to know where your money goes before you can begin to change financial direction.

• For This Week •

GET A little notebook and carry it with you at all times. Write down everything you spend—every dime in a parking meter, every postage stamp, every latte, every bag of groceries, every can of cat food—everything.

Don't try to change your spending—just pay attention to it. Don't judge or scold yourself. Just write it down.

At the end of the week, tally what you've spent. Divide it into categories—personal and business. Look at what you spent on your family. Notice what you spent on yourself. Pay special attention to any expenditures that seem especially big.

Also notice if there are things you are unwilling to spend any money on. Sometimes women spend too much money trying to make themselves feel better—while other women will spend *no* money on themselves because they feel unworthy. Both patterns indicate some self-esteem issues that need attending to.

WEEK 40

MEDITATE FOR AT LEAST FIVE MINUTES EACH DAY.

Meditation brings wisdom; lack of meditation leaves ignorance. Know well what leads you forward and what holds you back, and choose the path that leads to wisdom.

—The Buddha

The Buddha was not a god, he was not the messiah—he was a wise teacher whose wisdom is available to anyone from any faith. His understanding of the human mind is deeply insightful, profoundly wise, and extremely helpful to those of us who seek to understand ourselves better.

The Buddha taught that we all have a "monkey mind"—as if our minds were home to dozens of drunken monkeys, jumping around, screeching and chattering nonstop all day long. We're not all afflicted with ADD—we simply have normal human brains that keep up a nonstop stream of commentary, whether we like it or not. Some of these drunken monkeys echo things our parents taught us;

other monkey voices are those of our teachers, neighbors, friends, and religious authority figures; and still others are simply our own internal voices of doubt, fear, anxiety, hope, excitement, desire, worry, and much more. Needless to say, this cacophony of voices can drive us crazy if we don't understand it and know how to work with it.

That's where meditation comes in. Meditation is simply a quieting of the chorus of drunken monkeys—it involves taming our inner voices so that we can harness our minds' energy to make it work for us, rather than against us. Much as one would tame a wild stallion in order to ride him, we can tame our minds in order to focus our mental energy to become more successful and happy. Meditation is the way we tame our minds.

There are many schools of meditation, each teaching its own technique or style. For instance, Transcendental Meditation involves personal training with a TM teacher, who gives you a mantra to aid in your meditation. You sit twice a day, morning and afternoon, for twenty minutes each time, and silently repeat your mantra over and over again. As you do so, your mind calms down, your attention is focused on your mantra, and you seem to sink into a deep, restful state of consciousness, free from the chatter of drunken monkeys.

But you don't have to take TM training in order to meditate. Many schools of meditation teach you to simply follow your breath—in and out—slowly, patiently, softly, consistently. By focusing on your inbreathing and outbreathing, you focus on something very simple, thereby quieting your mind, freeing yourself from the drunken monkeys.

Considerable research has been conducted over the past forty years conclusively demonstrating the benefits of meditation: lowered blood pressure, reduced stress, better sleeping at night, fewer incidents of illness, increased levels of happiness, and heightened sense of well-being. In addition to the physical health benefits, many meditation practitioners claim that they've become more creative through regular daily meditation, as well as becoming more successful in their jobs and careers.

In short, meditation is not some woo-woo practice that only mystics and spiritual seekers do. Meditation has gone mainstream, with everyone from bankers, CEOs, sports figures, filmmakers, accountants, housewives, teachers, and just regular folks participating. If you're inclined to reject such things as meditation out of hand, I encourage you to give it a try before deciding whether or not it can help you with your self-care.

• For This Week •

MEDITATE JUST five minutes each day. Early morning is best—right after you wake up, before you launch into your day. Meditating in the morning—before you shower, have breakfast, read the paper, make lunch for the kids, or anything else—will help clear the clutter from your mind and begin your day refreshed and relaxed, no matter how you slept the night before.

If you can meditate longer—ten or fifteen minutes—great. But don't push it. As in all desires for enhanced personal self-care, start small, take baby steps, and go slowly. You want to build a healthy habit of meditating each day, to tame your drunken monkeys and focus your mind on what's important in your life.

If you want to read a book or listen to a CD on meditation, great. But you don't have to. You can simply sit on a comfy chair in a quiet place where no one will interrupt you, close your eyes, breathe in and out slowly and consistently, and focus your mind on following your breath. Buddhist Tonglen meditation teaches breathing meditation to transform negative feelings into positive. Breathe in your worries; breathe out relaxation. Breathe in your stress; breathe out serenity. Breathe in tension; breathe out healing.

Try it. You might like it.

WEEK 41

BUY YOURSELF SOME FRESH-CUT FLOWERS.

Bread feeds the body, indeed,
but flowers feed also the soul.
—The Koran

FRESH FLOWERS ARE one of Mother Nature's choicest treasures. Vibrant colors and luscious scents, in an amazing variety of shapes and sizes—everything about fresh flowers delights your senses, lifts your spirits, and pleases your mind. It's almost impossible not to smile when someone hands you a bouquet—or even just a single bloom.

But you don't have to wait for someone to give you flowers—you can give them to yourself. And they don't have to be fancy or expensive—a simple bunch of daisies will bring sunshine to a room far out of proportion to their cost. In the spring I like to buy a little bunch of small yellow daffodils from my local corner store—a whopping $1.29 buys me bright, buttery yellow flowers that keep me smiling for a week. Most supermarkets carry bunches of cut flowers that cost less than $5.00—small price to pay for the healthy benefits of having fresh, fragrant blooms in your home or office.

• For This Week •

BUY YOURSELF a bunch of fresh cut flowers, or a simple single bloom. Pick the kind of flower that most delights your senses. Some flowers, like orchids, are gorgeous but have no scent. Others, like gardenias, are both beautiful and laden with fragrance. Buy flowers that will nurture your spirit, but not break your bank account. If you have plenty of money, then a big bouquet of imported tropic blooms might be just the thing. If your budget is more modest, perhaps a bunch of tulips or short-stemmed roses or a handful of daisies would fill the bill.

Put the flowers where you will see them most often and where they will bring you refreshment when you need it most. Either home or office is fine. Place them where they will do you the most good—maybe even a flower in your hair.

WEEK 42

SEEK FORGIVENESS FROM PEOPLE YOU'VE HURT OR HARMED. MAKE AMENDS.

Guilt is anything you did and fear others to know about.

—Mohammad

GUILT IS A terrible and destructive burden. When we feel guilty about something we've done—or something we were supposed to do but didn't—it hurts our self-esteem. And if we have shaky self-esteem to begin with, guilt can be the thing that drives us over the edge into self-hatred. Whether we feel only a little guilty about hurting someone or enormously guilty for a serious damage we inflicted, it will continue to take its toll until we make amends for our transgression.

All the world's great religions preach the value of confession, atonement, amends, and restitution. Even if no one else knows of the harm you've done, *you* know it. And the harm you do yourself by keeping your guilty secret can be significant. Feeling bad about something you did to hurt someone, even unintentionally, will get in the way of your self-care.

Making amends benefits two people: It helps the person you hurt—it gives him or her closure, as well as the opportunity to forgive you—and it helps you. Even if the other person does not forgive you, you can still forgive yourself and free yourself of the guilt you've been carrying around.

You want to make amends for misdeeds from your past just as soon as you can muster the courage. You don't have to do them all at once. Start with just one.

• For This Week •

MAKE A list of all the people you've hurt or harmed in your life. Be honest with yourself. No one will see this list but you.

Making a complete list will enable you to measure how much guilt you're carrying around with you. The things you've done to hurt others might be "little things" like something you did as a child, or something rather impersonal like shoplifting as a teen, or something very personal like saying something mean or cruel to another person. Don't evaluate your transgressions—just list them. List them all. Keep your list in a safe place where others won't see it.

Review your list and pick one person to make amends to this week. Just one. Start there and see how you feel after you tell the person you're sorry you hurt him or her. It doesn't matter if that person forgives you or not. The point is for you to make a sincere effort to clean up any mistakes from your past, forgive yourself, and move into the future unencumbered by guilty secrets.

WEEK 43

TAKE CARE OF YOUR CAR.

The car has become a secular sanctuary for the individual, his shrine to the self, his mobile Walden Pond.

—Edward McDonagh, California sociologist

Here in Los Angeles where I live, "you are what you drive." Laugh if you will, but there's a kernel of truth in that—even if you don't live in L.A. The kind of car a person drives will tell you something about that person. It won't tell you *everything* about that person, but it will tell you something.

For instance, Warren Buffett, one of the world's richest men, drives an older car, a plain old sedan from one of the Big Three automakers. What does that tell us about Mr. Buffett? He is practical, down-to-earth, secure in who he is, and doesn't need to bolster his ego with a hot muscle car, like a Corvette, or a conspicuously pricey car, like a Rolls-Royce. His values and priorities determine the kind of car he chooses—and he's a guy who could afford anything.

If you value safety and reliability, you will choose a car that is well built and gets good safety ratings from *Consumer Reports* and strong reliability ratings from J. D. Power. If you think of yourself as youthful and sporty, you're likely to choose a jaunty car that reflects your self-image. If utility and practicality are your concerns, you'll choose some sort of minivan, SUV, station wagon, or truck for your transportation needs.

But whatever kind of vehicle you drive, how you take care of it also provides clues about who you are and how you regard yourself. Not taking good care of our wheels is often another way women fail to do what they know is good for them. Checking the oil regularly, checking the air pressure in the tires, getting the car into the mechanic for tune-ups, and keeping the vehicle washed and vacuumed are all ways we can take care of ourselves—or not.

• For This Week •

TAKE CARE of your wheels, so your wheels will take care of you. You're a woman on the go, and it's hard to get to where you want to be if you've neglected your car.

This week, wash your car or truck. Take it to a car wash or do it yourself (it's good exercise). It takes less than an hour and it can make a big difference in how you feel in your vehicle. Looking out through a sparkling clean windshield will make you feel like you can see forever—or at least to the end of the next block.

Just like taking a shower or bath makes you feel refreshed for the rest of the day, so will washing your car. Having a tidy interior makes driving a little bit more peaceful. You won't be rummaging around in the fast-food wrappers on the floor, or fumbling through all the stuff you've stuffed into your glove compartment.

Whether your car is old or new, whether the paint is shiny or dull, keeping it clean is a wonderful way to do something simple that is good for you.

WEEK 44

BUY OR MAKE A FIRST AID KIT.

It wasn't raining when Noah built the ark.

—Howard J. Ruff, author of *How to Prosper in the Coming Bad Years of the 21st Century*

EVERY PART OF the country has its natural dangers. The Midwest has tornadoes; the Southeast has hurricanes; the Northeast has violent nor'easter storms; the northern plains have subzero winters; the Southwest has scorching heat and drought; and here in California we have our earthquakes. Pick your poison—everybody has something to deal with, sooner or later.

We all know this, and yet most of us are unprepared when disaster strikes. Here in the Land of Shake & Bake, there is no "if" about earthquakes—there is only the question of "when." We all know the Big One is coming—

probably in our lifetimes. And yet, how many people are prepared for that day? Very few.

Every time we have an earthquake, the topic of preparedness is suddenly on everyone's lips. It's all over the news: "Is your family prepared?" Our intentions are good. We look at our loved ones and vow to put together an earthquake kit right away. But the road to hell is paved with good intentions, and I'd bet money that a good percentage of those intentions have to do with preparing for disasters. Somehow we never get around to it.

Many people are like my neighbor down the street. She's lived in her house for thirty years, and her home has been broken into eleven times. It wasn't until after the eleventh time that she finally installed a security system. She's a slow learner, for sure. And I'll bet a lot of us aren't any faster at learning how to take care of our safety and security needs!

Twenty years ago, the organization I worked for hosted a company-wide Safety Day for all employees. They conducted workshops, hired experts to answer our questions, and hosted vendors selling first aid kits and earthquake kits. I bought three of each—for my home, my car, and my office. I began keeping a blanket and bottles of water in the trunk of my car, along with a pair of running shoes, a sweatshirt and sweatpants (I call them my "earthquake clothes"), and a spare jacket.

I also put a bag of dry cat food in the trunk, just in case. I read someplace that bush pilots in Alaska keep a bag of dry cat food in their airplanes because the kibble is high in protein—humans can survive on it for a long time if they have to. Dry cat food also has a long shelf life, making it perfect for wilderness survival situations, when it may take many days for rescue teams to find you. Now, Los Angeles isn't Alaska—but in a disaster like a massive earthquake, terrorist attack, or widespread riots, we might have our own kind of urban wilderness. (Besides, I have six cats and a dog, so I want to be prepared for them, too.)

Doing what we know is good for us isn't only about the ordinary, day-to-day things we need to do. We must think about the unthinkable—and prepare, just in case.

It's been twenty years since I bought those first aid kits and earthquake kits for my car, home, and office. I update them periodically and replace dated items, but I've never had to use them. And that's fine with me. It was still money well spent. A disaster preparedness kit (whether for hurricane, tornado, fire, flood, or earthquake) is something you hope you never have to use. Like an insurance policy, a disaster kit is an excellent thing to have—whether or not you ever have to use it.

• For This Week •

START SIMPLE. Go to your local supermarket or drugstore and buy a first aid kit. (You can get a good basic one for $25.) Put it in the trunk of your car, along with several bottles of water, an old blanket, and a flashlight. That's a good start.

If you're committed to being even more prepared, buy first aid kits for your home and office, too. You can put your disaster supplies in an inexpensive backpack, so you can carry it easily if you need to—or in a small suitcase with wheels. Packages of dried fruit and nuts, protein bars, and bottles of water are all good things to include.

And be sure to include food for your pets, too—even if you don't want to eat the dry cat food yourself!

WEEK 45

TELL YOURSELF THE TRUTH ABOUT THE MEN IN YOUR LIFE.

I've learned that you can tell a lot about a person
by the way he or she handles these three things:
a rainy day, lost luggage, and tangled Christmas tree lights.

—Maya Angelou, poet, author, actress, professor

WHY DON'T WE pick the men we know are good for us? Now there's grist for the mill, for sure!

Dr. Pat Allen, author of *Getting to "I Do,"* says that the reason a woman picks the wrong men to fall in love with is: "Her picker is broken." Her picker—the intuition, the attraction, the chemistry that leads her to pick one man over others—is defective. Her childhood experiences, especially with her father (or other male caretakers), have conditioned her to choose men who cannot or will not be loving, protecting, cherishing partners to her.

This woman can walk into a room with a hundred men in it, and somehow her radar will find the one guy who is the *least* likely to give her what she needs and wants. She'll intuitively gravitate to the most troublesome guy in the room—bells and whistles will go off in her head and she'll light up like a Christmas tree. "That one!" she'll say, "That's the guy for me!" And she's off to the races—down the track to yet another bad relationship.

If this doesn't describe you and the men in your life, consider yourself blessed and skip to the next chapter. You're very fortunate, indeed, to know how to pick healthy men to fall in love with.

If you're not so fortunate—if you have a track record of getting involved with inappropriate men—the first thing to do is tell yourself the truth. If you've had lots of great relationships and one bad one, then you can probably write that off to the luck of the draw. But if you've had one bad relationship after another, it's time to look in the mirror and ask yourself, "What do all those men have in common?"

The answer is: you. What all those men have in common is the fact that *you* picked 'em! I know. You didn't want to hear that. It can be horrifying to realize that we do this to ourselves. The guys aren't doing it to us—we're the ones who do the picking!

If you ever hope to change your pattern of picking bad boys, married men, alcoholics and drug addicts, workaholics, emotionally unavailable men, abusive men, or dangerous men, the place to start is with yourself. Tell yourself the truth about yourself and the men in your life. And tell a trusted friend as well. Your best girlfriend, a good therapist, your priest or rabbi or spiritual teacher—confide in someone you respect and trust, someone who loves you and has your best interests at heart. Give up your secret pain—tell your truth about men.

• For This Week •

MAKE A list of all the significant males in your life, starting from childhood, right up to today. Include your dad, brothers, uncles, grandfathers, sons, male teachers, priests or rabbis, boyfriends, friends who happened to be male, lovers, husbands, bosses, male coworkers or neighbors, and any other important men in your life. Jot down a few notes about each one—adjectives, words that come to your mind, positive or negative feelings. Make your list as thorough and complete as you can. You're "cleaning house" with this assignment, so make sure you don't overlook any significant guys hidden away in the recesses of your mind.

When your list is complete, find some quiet time alone to read it to yourself. How do you feel as you go over the list? Write a bit about your feelings.

Finally, find someone you trust to read your list to. Make sure this is someone you trust absolutely. You are giving this person a very intimate inventory of your love life, and you want to ensure that you're in safe hands.

When you're finished, do something relaxing, quiet, nurturing. Take a bubble bath; go for a stroll on the beach or in a park; sit quietly in a cozy place with a scented candle or incense; curl up with your favorite quilt or comforter. Let your body relax in the aftermath of your emotional experience. Be gentle with yourself.

WEEK 46

ACKNOWLEDGE ALL THE DIFFERENT WAYS YOU AVOID DOING THE THINGS YOU KNOW ARE GOOD FOR YOU.

Cats are dangerous companions for writers
because cat watching is a near-perfect
method of writing avoidance.
—Dan Greenburg, humorist, novelist,
screenwriter, playwright

I AM A WRITER. And I have six cats, a dog, a rabbit, two cars, a modest two-story house, a big yard with a garden, a home-based business to run, and lots of great friends. My life is full: I exercise my body, walk the dog twice a day, scoop the poop from the cat litter boxes, do laundry, take care of the cars, go to the market, make phone calls, take phone calls, check the mail, check the e-mail, browse through the two newspapers that arrive every morning, run to the post office, call my eighty-year-old mom to see how she's doing, stop by the pet store for cat food and bunny pellets, find someone to clear the brush on my hillside, watch some TV, call the plumber to fix the leaky water heater, and on and on and on. I have *hundreds* of things that can interfere with my writing every day!

The other night I called my friend Sam Beasley because I was stuck with my writing. I had had great plans to start writing first thing in the morning, but oh, first I needed to deposit a check in the bank (always a good thing), and then I had to drop off a couple of prescriptions that needed refilling, and then I stopped to pick up some take-out chicken and salad, and by the time I got home and ate lunch, I was tired. "I donated blood yesterday," I remembered, "so no wonder I'm tired. I'll just take a little nap, then I'll start writing." But when I woke up, I felt lethargic: "I'm in no mood to write," I mumbled to no one in particular. I puttered around the house . . . and before I knew it, it was time for dinner and the evening news. My day was shot.

I picked up the phone. "Sam, I'm stuck!" I whined when he answered my call. I lamented pissing the day away, leaving myself with no energy for my book. "Can you help me get unstuck? I need to get back to my writing, but my mind wants to do anything *but* write."

Sam's response was reassuring—and amusing: "Well, isn't it interesting that you're writing a book about self-care? Let me ask you, is earning a living an important element in doing what you know is good for you?"

"Yes, of course," I said. Then I got the joke (sometimes I'm a little slow on the uptake, especially when the joke is on me). Here I was, in the middle of writing about self-care—and I let myself get distracted, to avoid taking care of myself! It was too funny—Sam and I both laughed.

"Okay, so enough laughing," Sam said. "Here's my suggestion for you. Look at all the different ways you avoid doing what's good for you. Start with this situation."

That's why Sam is my go-to guy for getting unstuck. I always have to have a go-to guy or gal when I write. Sometimes it's my editor; sometimes it's my coauthor; or sometimes it's a good friend.

Thanks, Sam, I needed that.

• For This Week •

MAKE A list of the ways you avoid taking care of yourself. Maybe it's procrastination; perhaps it's letting yourself get distracted; it might be always saying "yes" to family and friends when sometimes you want to say "no." Take an honest look at the variety of ways you avoid doing what's good for you.

Once you've got your list, ask yourself, "Are there people who support me in taking care of myself? Can I ask someone to be my go-to guy or go-to gal when I get off track? Do I know someone who cares for me enough to play that role?"

Being honest with yourself about how you sabotage your own well-being is a *huge* step in the right direction. Good for you!

Now keep your cell phone handy so you can call your go-to person to help when you get stuck.

IF YOU, OR SOMEONE YOU LOVE, IS STRUGGLING WITH AN ADDICTION, FIND A LOCAL SUPPORT GROUP.

You do anything long enough to escape the habit
of living until the escape becomes the habit.
—David Ryan, oft-quoted addiction expert

ADDICTION IS FAR more common than most people realize. Millions of men, women, and yes, even children are caught in a web of addiction—the harder they struggle to get free, the more their addiction entangles them. Some people's addictions are relatively easy to spot—frequent intoxication, obesity, anorexia, smoking, and the highly public drug and alcohol addictions that ravage lost souls on the mean streets of our cities.

But many more people wrestle with their demons privately, indulging in secret, hiding their guilt and shame—all the while putting up a respectable front for the rest of the world. Compulsive shoppers, bulimics who gorge themselves then purge to stay thin, Internet porn addicts, compulsive gamblers, prescription drug abusers, sex addicts, compulsive hoarders, and closet alcoholics are all around us—driving on our freeways, working in our offices, teaching in our schools, caring for others in our hospitals, living in our neighborhoods, and yes, sitting around our family dinner tables. Addicts usually indulge in secret, making it hard to know who's in trouble, often until it's too late.

Addicts are not bad people—they are not morally inferior or lacking in intelligence, talent, creativity, ambition, or love for family and friends. Addicts are, by and large, people for whom life is stressful—they feel like their nerves are on the *outside* of their skin, not inside. Addicts have low or shaky self-esteem—their inability to be comfortable in their own skin is what drives them to seek relief in a substance or an activity. The bottom line: Life is painful and they just want to feel better. They reach out for something to take for their comfort and it works. So they do it again. And again. And again. Because the anesthetic effect of their "drug of choice"—be it booze, sugar, gambling, TV, sex, pills, or work—wears off and they have to do it some more. It doesn't take long before their little indulgence now and then turns into a regular habit—a habit they can't break. Their best friend (alcohol, shopping, food, fill-in-the-blank) has become their slave master.

If you are worried that you might be addicted to

something, seek help. Search the Internet or open your local phone book and look up the organizations that can help you: Alcoholics Anonymous, Overeaters Anonymous (for overeating, undereating, or bingeing and purging), Gamblers Anonymous, Narcotics Anonymous, Debtors Anonymous (for compulsive shoppers and other forms of money madness), Nicotine Anonymous, Sex and Love Addicts Anonymous, among others.

If the suspected addict is a spouse, parent, child, sibling, or other family member—or a friend or someone you love—check out Al-Anon, for families of addicts. If you grew up in a family with addict parents, look for Adult Children of Alcoholics (ACA). If you're in a love relationship with an addict, find Co-Dependents Anonymous (CODA).

Twelve-step groups aren't for everyone, but they do have the highest success rate of any medical or therapeutic treatment today. If twelve-step groups aren't your cup of tea, there are therapists around the country who specialize in helping people with compulsive/addictive problems. In addition, treatment centers with both inpatient and outpatient programs are available in different price ranges.

Many excellent books have been written on addictions of all types. You can seek help in the privacy of your own home by reading books, as well as by searching the virtual treasure trove of material available on the Internet.

• For This Week •

CHANCES ARE, someone you love, someone in your family, or one of your close friends is an addict. Perhaps the addict is you. Educate yourself about the symptoms of addiction. You can't help anyone else—or yourself—if you don't know there's a problem.

Visit one or more of these Web sites to learn more:

www.alcoholics-anonymous.org (for problems with alcohol)

www.oa.org (for problems with food, weight, overeating, undereating, purging)

www.debtorsanonymous.org (for money problems, compulsive shopping, underearning, excessive credit card debt, business debt)

www.slaafws.org (for relationship problems)

www.saa-recovery.org (for sex addicts)

www.codependents.org (for anyone from a dysfunctional family)

www.al-anon.org (for families of addicts and alcoholics)

www.al-anon.alateen.org (for teenagers who have an addict or alcoholic parent)

www.nicotine-anonymous.org (for smokers who want to quit)

www.adultchildren.org (for adults who grew up in alcoholic families)

WEEK 48

MAKE A GOD BOX.

You can tell the size of your God
by looking at the size of your worry list.
The longer your list, the smaller your God.
—Anonymous

A FEW YEARS AGO, I heard a wonderful story about a guy named George who decided to stretch a cable across Niagara Falls and then ride his bicycle on the cable, going from one side of the roaring waterfall to the other. A crowd gathered as George prepared for his ride. People began to shout their support and encouragement: "You can do it, George!" "We believe in you!" "Go for it!" "We believe you can do it!" The crowd grew larger, their chants of support escalated, and George set off on his bike on the cable across the crashing waterfall.

When he reached the other side, the crowd erupted in

wild applause. "Hurray for George!" "We knew you could do it!" "We believed in you!"

George turned around and rode his bicycle back across the falls. The crowd was ecstatic.

George beamed at the crowd and then announced, "I'm going to do it again. Who wants to come with me?"

The crowd grew silent as everyone shrank from his invitation. Then a little girl stepped forward, looked up at George, and said, "I'll go with you."

George smiled, leaned forward, picked up the little girl, and put her on the handlebars of his bike.

The crowd erupted in fury. "Stop him, someone stop him!" "Where are the girl's parents?" "Don't do it, George. You have no right to take her with you!" "Someone should call the police!" But before anyone could stop him, George set out again, riding on the cable spanning the roaring falls.

The crowd fell silent—everyone holding their breath. And when George reached the other side with the little girl, they broke into cheers.

As before, George promptly turned his bike around and rode back across the waterfall one last time.

When he reached safety, he lifted the little girl down from his handlebars and kissed her on top of her head. The crowd gathered around the little girl. "Why did you do that?" they wanted to know.

The little girl looked up at the sea of faces surrounding her and replied: "All of you *believed* in George, but I *trusted* him. He's my daddy."

Ninety-eight percent of Americans say they believe in God. But *belief* is different from *trust.* Our U.S. dollars and cents proclaim, "In God we trust." But . . . do we really?

What is the nature of your relationship with God? Do you believe God exists but you don't trust Him to take care of you? Do you trust God to take care of you? Are you uncertain of your belief and/or trust?

Spend some time this week reflecting on your relationship with God, or whatever you call it—the Divine, the Holy, the Numinous, the Universe, Gaia, Goddess, Mother/Father/God, or . . .

• For This Week •

MAKE A God box. A God box is a container into which you place your worries, cares, concerns, resentments, and problems. It can be as simple as a shoe box, with a slit cut in the top (like some of us made in grade school for our valentines). It can be a lidded box that you decorate with paint, collage, images, and/or words. Your God box is very personal, so it can look like whatever you want it to look like. For instance, mine is a lovely painted gourd with a lid. It's lined with soft tie-dyed velvet, and has carved designs on the outside.

Whenever you have a fear or worry that you want to turn over to God, simply write it on a small piece of paper, fold it up, and say a short prayer telling God that you're turning the problem over to Him. Put the paper in your God box and let it go. That's it. You're done. Go about the rest of your day knowing that you surrendered your fear, worry, or problem to someone who can take care of it for you.

WEEK 49

DO WHAT YOU LOVE.

If you hear a voice within you saying,
"You are not a painter,"
then by all means paint . . .
and that voice will be silenced.
—Vincent van Gogh, Dutch painter

OVER THE YEARS I've learned that there isn't a job you can't lose, a house that can't burn down, a person who can't die or leave you, money that can't be lost or stolen, a family that can't be wiped out, or treasures that can't be destroyed. In short, there is no security in external things—so I might as well do what I love.

If you spend your life looking for security in people, places, or things, sooner or later you will be sorely disappointed. For as the Buddha pointed out over 2,500 years ago, all is impermanent. Things come and things go—that is the nature of things. There isn't a person in your life who won't ultimately leave you. People die, get divorced, become estranged, or just drift apart—everyone leaves.

So then what's the point? The point is simply to live your life. Do what you love. Don't live your life for others' expectations or approval—live it for yourself. Be the very best *you* that you can be. That's your primary job in life. Do what you love.

• For This Week •

ASK YOURSELF a few simple questions:

- If I knew I had only one year to live, how would I be living it?
- If money were no object, where would I live, and with whom?
- If I could design my ideal job/career, what would it be?
- What are my gifts and my talents?
- What do I want to be remembered for when I die?

See if the answers to these questions give you some new insights into what you want to do to live your own best life.

WEEK 50

ENROLL IN A PERSONAL DEVELOPMENT CLASS.

There came a time when the risk
to remain tight in the bud was more painful
than the risk it took to blossom.
—Anaïs Nin, French-born diarist, author

WHEN I WENT to college, one of the counselors gave me some really good advice. I didn't know what I wanted to major in, so he said, "Just go through the course catalog and sign up for whatever interests you. As you get into the classes, you'll find that some won't be what you thought they were—drop them. And some of the teachers you won't like—drop them, too. Pick other classes to take their place. You'll love some of your classes, and others you'll lose interest in. Over time, by process of elimination, you'll zero in on what you really love. Bingo! You'll have your major!"

What a wonderful way to discover one's passion, one's

path in life, one's career. I'm so grateful to that counselor, though I never even knew his name. (Wisdom and sage advice come to us from all sorts of people, if we're willing to listen.) I followed his counsel and, within a couple of years, I found my major—sociology.

But learning doesn't stop when we graduate from school. That's why they call it "commencement"—it's a beginning, not an end. No matter what your age, you want to keep learning—for in learning you stay curious, interested, involved, and engaged. You might want to go back to school—for fun, to find a new hobby, to explore other career options, to train for a new job, or to meet new people who share your interests. You can take personal development classes in psychology and/or spirituality, to understand yourself better. Or maybe you want to keep up your learning through books on tape, audio seminars, DVDs, or self-help books.

The point is, doing the things you know are good for you includes stimulating your brain with continuous life-long learning. Your brain cells will thank you.

• For This Week •

CONSIDER ENROLLING in a personal development class. Check out what's available at your local community college. See what the high school has available in terms of adult education in the evenings. Find out what workshops and seminars are offered at your church or synagogue. Visit your local YMCA and see what kinds of exercise classes they have. If there is a state college or university nearby, see if they have a college of continuing education or an extension program. Hospitals often offer lectures and workshops on nutrition, healthy aging, and disease prevention—as well as living with certain chronic conditions like diabetes. Check out your local bookstore for book signings, author events, lectures, and short classes. The Sierra Club offers workshops on nature-related topics. Other nonprofit organizations also offer lectures, seminars, and workshops that might be of interest to you. Therapists and spiritual teachers often offer their own public workshops, too.

There is a veritable feast of information, instruction, and inspiration all around you—pick what you like and have fun!

WEEK 51

USE THE PHRASE "UP UNTIL NOW . . ." TO CREATE OPENINGS FOR CHANGE.

Habit is habit, and not to be flung out the window . . .
but coaxed downstairs one step at a time.
—Mark Twain, humorist, author

I WAS HAVING lunch with my friend Anita Goldstein one day. I was complaining to her about my frustration with my procrastination, and the pressure I put myself under by waiting until the last minute to get things done.

"I have a hard time getting started . . . I have a million things to do other than the thing I most need to do," I said.

"Up until now," Anita interrupted.

"Huh? What?" I asked, surprised.

"Up until now," she repeated. "Every time you hear yourself making some blanket statement like that, I'd suggest that you add those three words, 'up until now.' Every time you do that, you're making a break with the past.

You're giving yourself permission to change. Just because you were a certain way in the past, does not mean that you necessarily have to be that way today . . . or in the future. 'Up until now' acknowledges what was true in the past, but it also gives you freedom for something different in the future."

"Okay," I replied. "Up until now I have procrastinated starting projects."

"How does it feel when you say that?" she asked me.

"Different . . . and awkward," I said. "Now I'm not sure how I feel about needing to dillydally before I get started."

"Great!" she said. "Just be with that. Consider the possibility that maybe you've changed. Just because you were a certain way in the past, doesn't mean that you're still that way."

"Okay," I agreed.

"And remember that phrase, 'up until now,' and use it any time you hear yourself making some kind of absolute judgment or statement about yourself . . . see if it makes a difference," she concluded.

That conversation occurred about twenty years ago, and I can tell you that it has made a *huge* difference in my life. It has given me freedom from the tyranny of the past, and opened up new possibilities for change. When I catch myself making pronouncements about myself, especially negative pronouncements . . . "I'm disorganized . . . I'm easily distracted . . . I don't have a good memory for names . . .

I'm impulsive . . ." I interrupt myself and correct myself midsentence: "*Up until now* I've been disorganized." In so doing, I give myself the freedom to change.

Language is powerful. My friend Anita taught me that three little words can transform my life. I can give myself freedom by keeping the past in the past, and not letting the past dictate my future.

• For This Week •

I'LL GIVE you the same assignment that Anita gave me: This week, whenever you hear yourself making blanket statements or absolute pronouncements about yourself, catch yourself and change your language. Insert those three simple words, "up until now." See if it doesn't begin to change your feelings and attitude about who you are. Language is powerful. Use it to your advantage.

WEEK 52

OWN YOUR ACCOMPLISHMENTS. ENJOY THE "NEW YOU" YOU'RE BECOMING.

If we all did the things we are capable of,
we would astound ourselves.
—Thomas Edison, scientist, inventor

YEARS AGO, WHEN I was a corporate manager, I had to give performance appraisals to the people I managed. I always asked them to write out a self-appraisal first, so that when we sat down together, it would be a two-way conversation. I invited each employee to tell me about his or her self-appraisal first, before I gave him or her my appraisal.

Over the years of doing these performance reviews, I noticed an interesting trend: My best performers always rated themselves lower than I rated them, and my poor performers always rated themselves better than I rated them. In other words, there was often a gap between how people saw themselves and how I saw them. This discovery was fascinating!

Here's my theory about women who don't do the things they know are good for them: These women are the best women—they are talented, creative, smart, attractive, loving, kind, resourceful, hardworking, honest, generous, amazing women. And if you're reading this book, chances are *you* are one of these best women!

But you don't always see yourself this way. You don't see how good you really are. But don't take my word for it. Check it out for yourself.

• For This Week •

MAKE A list of all the things you're proud of in your life. These might be family things like raising well-adjusted kids, or personal growth accomplishments like going back to college, or personal successes such as overcoming a major phobia or fear. It's easy to overlook how much we have done in our lives because our minds want to keep reminding us about what's still missing. But dig deep. Spend some time reflecting on your accomplishments, successes, and achievements. Jot down a list of your talents and skills. Make note of your personal and professional strengths.

Add new items to the list as you begin to remember more and more good things you're proud of. And read this list any time self-doubt or insecurity rear their ugly heads. You're terrific and you and I both know it. It's just that sometimes you forget. So I'm here to remind you.

Section III

WHAT?

WHAT BRINGS ABOUT SUCCESSFUL, LONG-TERM, PERSONAL CHANGE?

It's never too late to become
what you might have been.
—George Eliot (Mary Anne Evans, who
wrote under a man's name)

You've now completed fifty-two lessons in gradually, lovingly retraining yourself on many levels—emotional, physical, spiritual, financial, psychological, and social. What's next? Where do you go from here? How do you maintain the changes you've made so far? How do you continue to cultivate self-care and self-love in your daily life?

This is where many of us have a hard time . . . we can make changes for a short while, but over time we often slip back into old habits. Very human. Completely understandable. So I want to provide you with more ideas, suggestions, and ways to continue your success in doing the things you know are good for you.

This final section of the book is designed to show you how to build on the gains you've made, continuing to make strides, in the months and years ahead.

By understanding yourself, as well as understanding how people change, you will be in a great position to continue closing the gap between what you *know* and what you *do* in terms of self-care.

Above all, you want to set yourself up to be successful. Don't return to riding in the back of your own bus ever again. Stay in the driver's seat—where you belong.

PERSONAL CHANGE TIP #1

LEARN HOW YOUR MIND WORKS, THEN PUT IT TO WORK FOR YOUR HIGHEST AND BEST GOOD.

The mind is everything.
What you think you become.
—The Buddha

THE BUDDHA WAS the smartest psychologist I've ever read—his keen insights into human nature are extraordinarily helpful to anyone who wants to understand why people do what they do. Over 2,500 years ago, the Buddha taught his followers how the human mind works.

Every day, you have hundreds of thousands of thoughts; these thoughts are expressed each day in tens of thousands of words (some spoken out loud, others in self-talk); these words lead to thousands of feelings; these feelings stimulate you to take hundreds of actions; these actions develop into a few dozen habits; these habits form your character; and your character becomes your destiny. Literally, *you become what you think about.*

The Buddha may have been the first to point this out, but since his day, countless teachers, spiritual leaders, and successful people in many fields have emphasized this critical key to living a happy, fulfilled life. The Bible states: "As a man thinketh in his heart so is he." Mahatma Gandhi, who led India to independence through nonviolence, pointed out, "Man often becomes what he believes himself to be." Philosopher Henry David Thoreau wrote, "Live your beliefs and you can turn the world around." Similarly, poet Ralph Waldo Emerson wrote: "That which dominates our imaginations and our thoughts will determine our lives, and our character." Famed architect Frank Lloyd Wright agreed: "The thing always happens that you really believe in; and the belief in a thing makes it happen." Cosmetics maven Mary Kay Ash concurs: "You can go as far as your mind lets you. What you believe, remember, you can achieve."

Many of today's experts and authors echo this essential understanding of the power of our minds: Stephen R. Covey, author of the perennial bestseller *Seven Habits of Highly Effective People*, says: "The environment you fashion out of your thoughts, your beliefs, your ideals, your philosophy is the only climate you will ever live in." James Allen, author of the timeless classic *As a Man Thinketh*, wrote: "The outer conditions of a person's life will always be found to reflect their inner beliefs." Maxwell Maltz, author of the groundbreaking book *Psycho-Cybernetics*, asserted that "the self image is a 'premise,' a base, or a foundation upon which your entire personality, your behavior, and even your circumstances are built." Mark Victor Hansen, coauthor of the *Chicken Soup for the Soul®* series, echoes the Buddha when he says: "Your belief determines your action and your action determines your results; but first you have to believe." Napoleon Hill, author of *Think and Grow Rich*, wrote, "The reason man may become the master of his own destiny is because he has the power to influence his own subconscious mind." Motivational speaker Zig Ziglar says, "You have to 'be' before you can 'do' and 'do' before you can 'have.'"

Playwright George Bernard Shaw wrote, "Life isn't about finding yourself. Life's about creating yourself." Talk show queen Oprah Winfrey says, "I know for sure that what we dwell on is who we become." And years ago, automotive pioneer Henry Ford said, "Whether you think you can or think you can't, you're right." Even our children's books teach tots about the power of beliefs: "I think I can, I think I can," puffs the Little Engine That Could.

All these very smart, very wise, very successful people are telling us the same thing: What you think about is what you become.

So how do we harness the power of our minds to help us do more of the things we know are good for us? We begin by thinking thoughts that are good for us. We begin by creating a mental picture of what we want in our lives. I'll give you a personal example.

A number of years ago, I had a lunch meeting with University of Southern California professor Warren H. Schmidt. My boss at the time had told me to contact Dr. Schmidt to see if he would teach some classes in our professional development program for USC employees. As our lunch conversation progressed and I learned more about Dr. Schmidt, I thought to myself, "I want to be like him when I grow up." He was a published author with *Harvard Business Review* articles to his credit, a poet and writer of charming parables, an accomplished filmmaker with an Academy Award under his belt, and he was supremely talented in the classroom.

About ten years later, I recalled that luncheon meeting and I suddenly realized that I was now doing all the things I had admired in Professor Schmidt: I was skillfully teaching corporate seminars, I had learned to write parables and poetry, I had become a published author, and I was now making my parables into films. "Wow, I got what I wanted," I said to myself. "Isn't that great?"

That wasn't the only time I had such an experience. I once met an interesting couple through our common interest in art, who invited me to their home for dinner one evening. When I walked into their home, I felt like I was walking into an art gallery. Everything was beautiful—they had the most eclectic, interesting, unusual collection of paintings, sculptures, furniture, fabric, colors, textures, and designs I'd ever seen. I loved it!

Some years later, I was curled up with a good book at home on a rainy day. I took a break from my reading and let my attention wander. As I gazed around my living room, I realized that there was beautiful art everywhere—on the walls, on the stereo cabinet, on the fireplace mantel, on end tables—and some pieces of furniture, like the tile coffee table, were works of art in themselves. Then I remembered that couple whose home I had so admired. "Hmmm, I got what I wanted—again," I reflected.

I could give you many more examples of how this has worked in my own life. Here's how I describe it to friends: Occasionally I meet someone who's doing something, or who has something, that I want in my own life. I know I want it because it resonates with me—it's a vibration of energy I feel. I get excited, interested, enthused, almost captivated. My mind is telling me, "Ooooh, I like that," and my body responds with increased heart rate and quickened pulse. I am all eyes and ears, eager to take it in—every detail. It's as if I have a camera in my head and my brain takes a snapshot of whatever it is that has captured my attention.

Then I take that mental snapshot and metaphorically tack it up on the walls of my mind—I've captured an image of what I want and now I own it, mentally and emotionally.

Then I just go about my business. The snapshot is still in my mind, but I don't have to make an action plan, do a lot of hard work, or try to control things or other people. I simply hold the vision. And I go about living my day-to-day life.

Over time, my subconscious finds a way to make this snapshot manifest in my life. It doesn't have a fixed timetable. I can't control or predict when it will show up. But I know that it will. The positive energy I feel when I think about what I want is like a magnet. Getting what I want in life is about "pull energy" not "push energy." My mental images, and the positive feelings associated with them, create a powerful force that draws more of what I want into my life.

I first had these kinds of experiences when I was a teenager—long before I read any of the authors I quoted earlier in this chapter. I had never heard of the Law of Attraction, or the magic of believing, or psycho-cybernetics, or any of the other terms people use to refer to this process. All I knew was that this was how my mind worked.

It wasn't until many years later that I began to read and hear other people describe what I had experienced in my own life for many years. They wrote books about it; they taught classes about it. I was happy to learn that there was a name for what I had been experiencing.

"So how is this relevant to doing the things we know are good for us?" you might ask.

It has everything to do with what's good for us. If we can control our thoughts, focus our attention, and manifest things in our lives—jobs, houses, cars, lovers, money, art, people, and possessions—then we can certainly manifest a high level of self-care as well. We simply use what we know about how our minds work to channel our thoughts and become the self-respecting, self-loving, self-accepting women we want to be.

It's only hard if you want it to be hard. It's simple and easy if you want it to be. Let go of your attachment to it being hard. And let go of your story about self-care being selfish. You get to decide what you want for yourself—in self-care, as in everything else.

Create a picture in your mind: What would "doing the things I know are good for me" look like? Do you see yourself doing yoga? Eating fruits and vegetables? Getting massages? Having a nice, fat savings account? Being with a man who cherishes you? Having a job that challenges and excites you? Having a healthy, fit body? Enjoying lots of energy?

Remember, focus on what you *do* want, not what you don't want. It's okay to *glance* at negative things, but just glance, don't look for very long. You want to aim all your attention and energy at what you do want for your personal self-care.

When you meet or see women who are taking good care of themselves, get out your mental camera and take a "photo" of them. Tack these mental images to the walls of your mind. Surround yourself with positive images of women who love themselves, women who do what they know is good for them. These women are now your mentors—they are a vision of what's possible for you, too.

Use the power of your mind to create the kind of future you'd love to live into.

PERSONAL CHANGE TIP #2

STUDY HOW PEOPLE BRING ABOUT POSITIVE CHANGES IN THEIR LIVES.

We do not grow absolutely, chronologically. We grow sometimes in one dimension, and not in another; unevenly. We grow partially. We are relative. We are mature in one realm, childish in another. The past, present, and future mingle and pull us backward, forward, or fix us in the present. We are made up of layers, cells, constellations.

—Anaïs Nin, French-born diarist, author

MANY YEARS AGO, I asked a therapist if he thought people could change. "Of course people can change," he replied. "If they couldn't, therapy would be useless. Personal change is possible, but not easy. Doing therapy with people who want to change is like dealing with a baby riding an elephant. The baby is the intellectual part—the elephant is the emotional part. It's easy to get the baby to change direction, but it's harder to move that elephant." If you've ever tried to change something about yourself—a bad habit, a character defect, or a personality trait—you're probably nodding in agreement as you read his words.

I'm sure you've heard it said that "people don't like change." But that's not entirely true. People do not like change that is imposed on them by others. We don't like change that we didn't decide to make for ourselves—like having your department at work reorganized, or your son announcing that he's getting married to someone you don't like, or needing to buy a new car because your old one finally bit the dust, or experiencing the physical and mental aspects of aging. We don't like those changes one bit. They weren't our idea and we can't control them. That's the real truth—we don't like feeling out of control. That's why we often react badly to change.

But there are plenty of changes we make that we *do* like: We change our hairstyle; we apply for a new job and get it; we decide to go back to school; we decide to buy a new home; we purchase a new car; we change political parties; we take up a new sport or hobby; and many more. If it's a change that we instigate because we want to, we like change just fine.

But even when we want to, not all changes are as easy as getting a new hairstyle or taking a personal development class. Sometimes we want very much to change, but we just can't seem to do it. We want to lose weight, but those pesky pounds just won't come off. We want to change our spending habits, but it seems too hard to save money. We want to be in healthy relationships, but we keep attracting loser guys. Anyone who's tried to make such changes knows how difficult it can be.

So how *do* people bring about successful changes in these aspects of their lives? That's the $64,000 question!

Fortunately for us, many therapists, researchers, and professors are also interested in this question. Published studies shed some light on the process by which people bring about positive change in themselves.

Notable among these studies is research by Drs. James Prochaska, John Norcross, and Carlo Diclemente—they studied more than a thousand people who were "successful self-changers." By examining the change process in this large group of people, the researchers saw consistent patterns, enabling them to discern a six-stage program for change. Prochaska, Norcross, and Diclemente believe that "the secret to supported change lay in the knowledge and experience of those people who were able to initiate and maintain change themselves. . . . Their underlying thesis is that if you can understand where you are in the change process, you can 'create a climate where positive change can occur, maintain motivation, turn setbacks into progress, and make new beneficial habits a permanent part of your life.'"*

---

* Prochaska, James, John Norcross, and Carlo Diclemente. "Changing for Good." Positive Workplace Alliance (copyright © 2006 by Levy Davis), http://www.positiveworkplace.com/files/Abstract%20Change%20Prochaska.pdf (accessed 2006).

These are the six stages that successful self-changers go through:

1. **Precontemplation**—You're not even aware of the need for change. You're oblivious to your problem. Perhaps in denial.
2. **Contemplation**—The lightbulb goes on and you realize that something's wrong and you need, or want, to change. You start thinking about changing yourself. Perhaps you discuss it with others.
3. **Preparation**—You start to talk openly about the change you want to make. You do some research and think about various options and approaches to bringing about the desired change in yourself. You make a decision or commitment to change.
4. **Action**—You get your rear in gear and start doing something to bring about the change you seek.
5. **Maintenance**—You've made the change in yourself and now your task is to keep it up over the long haul.
6. **Termination**—The new behavior is so firmly established that you don't need to think or do much about it anymore. (At this point you may start the process all over again with another aspect of yourself you'd like to change.)

The change process is almost never linear—no surprise to those of us who have tried to change our behavior (eating habits, exercise, relating to men, clutter in our homes, spending habits, etc.). The journey to personal change often occurs in fits and starts, with two steps forward, followed by one step back.

Prochaska et al. say that self-changers spiral through these six stages, occasionally recycling through prior stages. Some people may have to go back again and again before they finally succeed. "Recycling gives us opportunities to learn. Action followed by relapse is far better than no action at all. People who take action and fail in the next month are twice as likely to succeed over the next six months than those who don't take any action at all. . . . In fact, there is some evidence that it may be more efficient to apply processes to more than one problem at a time, rather than trying to change problem behaviors one by one."* They conclude: "Our view is that change is often circular and difficult."** Gee, no kidding!

But many of their findings were encouraging:

- "Individuals who believe that they have the autonomy to change their lives are more likely to act successfully than those who are given limited choice."
- "People are more likely to be successful in their change attempts when they are given two choices

---

* *Ibid.*

** *Ibid.*

of how to pursue change rather than one; the success rate increases with three or more choices. Your motivation to change increases; your commitment becomes stronger; and you become more able to free yourself from your problem."

And my personal favorite:

- "Self-changers are just as successful in their efforts to change as those individuals who choose to enter therapy."*

In other words, you don't have to spend a fortune on therapists, psychiatrists, and/or medication in order to bring about positive changes in yourself.

I should also point out that while most personal change is incremental—unfolding in stages—there are people who change dramatically, suddenly, triggered by a significant emotional event or an epiphany. Probably all of us can think of someone we know who was suddenly transformed—becoming almost a different person. The biblical story of Saul traveling the road to Tarsus, who experienced a spiritual awakening, transforming him into the apostle Paul, is an ancient example of such a change. A conversion experience, a brush with mortality, the

---

* *Ibid.*

death of a loved one, witnessing the birth of your child, confronting a personal crisis, having a powerful dream or vision—any of these things can trigger profound change in a person.

And sometimes the transformative event comes quietly—Siddhartha Gautama meditating under the bodhi tree until he achieved enlightenment, becoming the Buddha, is a good example. Revelations and epiphanies can come unexpectedly in simple moments of daily life—savoring a sunset, walking in the desert, gazing into the eyes of a loved one, tasting a juicy ripe fruit, holding your sleeping child, or in times of prayer and meditation.

In short, personal change can be revolutionary—but more often it is *evolutionary*. We are more likely to change ourselves with many small steps than we are with one giant leap. If you're fortunate enough to have a spiritual experience relieve you of a character defect, congratulations! Enjoy your transformation.

But chances are, closing the gap between what you *know* is good for you and what you *do* about it will be a much slower process, with spirals, detours, slips, lapses, steps forward followed by stumbles backward.

Be patient with yourself. Trust that the process you're going through is normal. Be kind to yourself. Change, even when you want it, can be difficult to bring about. Be compassionate toward yourself. Show the same love and gentleness you would show a puppy that you're trying to train. And forgive yourself when you backslide. Trust that lapses are part of the process, too.

Learn all you can by watching other people who have been successful at bringing about personal changes. Read research on the change process. Pay attention only to experts who practice what they preach in terms of radical self-care.

Above all, love yourself every step of the way. Love your teachers, love the learning, love the process of change, and love yourself. Easier said than done, of course. But give it a shot—what have you got to lose but your frustration, disappointment, and unhappiness?

PERSONAL CHANGE TIP #3

COAX YOURSELF THROUGH THE "I DON'T WANNA" FEELINGS.

No matter how big or soft or warm your bed is, you still have to get out of it.

—Grace Slick, lead singer, Jefferson Airplane

THIS IS ONE of the biggest obstacles most people face in doing the things they know are good for them. It's true for me, too. I hate to think of all the times I didn't do what I knew was good for me because, simply, "I don't wanna."

I don't *wanna* exercise; I don't *wanna* balance my checkbook; I don't *wanna* give up sweets; I don't *wanna* date the boring nice guy—I want the exciting bad boy. Sometimes it seems like life is just one "I don't wanna" after another . . . and I don't like it. And I'd wager money that you don't either!

So I look at other areas of my life where the "I don't wanna" comes up as well. Motherhood, for instance, is full of "I don't wanna." I don't want to get up in the middle of the night for the umpteenth time to try to calm an inconsolable baby; I don't want to go to watch yet another soccer game; and I certainly don't want to help with homework. (I did my share of homework when I was in school; why should I have to help you with yours?) But I did it all anyway, despite the fact that I didn't want to. Parenthood involves thousands of things we don't want to do. But we do them anyway. Why? Is there a clue that I can apply to self-care?

Think about work—there's another arena chock-full of "I don't wanna." There aren't enough pages for me to list all the things I've done for a paycheck that I didn't want to do. But I did them anyway. Why? Any clues here?

Consider friendships—how often have we done things for (or with) our friends that we really didn't want to do? Parties we attended out of obligation; requests to which we said "yes" when we wanted to say "no"; favors for friends that were totally inconvenient. But we did them anyway. Why? What can we learn from this?

This question is tied into some of the chapters earlier in this book. It's a question of managing our own motivation—one of the hardest things we have to do in life. How do we keep ourselves motivated to do the things we know are good for us, *especially* when we don't want to?

First, remember the rule I gave you earlier in this book: *You're not allowed to beat yourself up*. No matter what. Whether or not you give in to the "I don't wanna," you're not allowed to beat yourself up.

Second, acknowledge the "I don't wanna." Accept the fact that it's there and it's dragging you down. Okay. Don't fight with it—you'll only give it power. Just notice it.

Third, use what you've learned about your own motivation to see if you can find creative solutions to "I don't wanna."

For instance, since most women will easily do for others what we often won't do for ourselves, find a way to make positive self-care something you do for the other people in your life. Lose some weight because you want to live to see your grandkids grow up. Put your makeup on because you want to be attractive to your husband or boyfriend. Straighten out your finances because you don't want your kids to have a mess to clean up when you die.

Recently, I read about the results of new research on what helps people quit smoking. (If you didn't know it, nicotine is probably *the* most addictive substance there is—rated as more addictive than heroin, crack cocaine, methamphetamines, and alcohol by physicians and other addiction specialists.) The research conclusively demonstrated that *guilt* is the most effective tool for smokers who want to quit.

Now, I'm not an advocate of guilt—it's generally a debilitating, unhelpful emotion. So I read more about this smoking research to see whether guilt might have a positive aspect after all.

One group of smokers was asked questions like: "Don't you want to be around to watch your kids grow up?" or

"Do you know how devastated your husband will be if you die from lung cancer?" or "Aren't you interested in living long enough to see your grandchildren born?" These smokers had a much higher success rate of quitting smoking than the other groups, in which smokers were asked questions like, "Don't you want to be healthy?" or "Do you want to live longer? If you quit smoking, you'll have a much longer life." In short, researchers found that feeling guilty about how smoking affects loved ones is much more effective than simply considering the harmful effects of smoking on oneself.

We talked in an earlier chapter about enrolling a friend to be your self-care action buddy. That's a great way to get through a bout of "I don't wanna"—you'll often show up for your buddy when you won't show up for yourself.

You can pay money for self-care—paying for something often gets people to show up when they might otherwise bail out. Hiring a personal trainer who is waiting for you at an appointed time each week is one option. Paying in advance for a ten-week yoga class is more likely to get you there than paying week by week. Money isn't always a surefire guarantee that you'll follow through—but it does increase the probability that you'll keep your commitment to yourself.

In short, use what you've learned about yourself so far to gently coax and cajole yourself through the "I don't wannas" that are bound to come up along the way. They're normal. Everyone has them. You're not alone. Some people are able to just suit up and show up anyway, regardless of their "I don't wannas"—others have a harder time getting over the hump of resistance that holds us back.

Be gentle with yourself. Listen to the "I don't wanna" and see if it's trying to tell you something important. Maybe there's something you need to learn about yourself—something only "I don't wanna" can teach you.

PERSONAL CHANGE TIP #4

PAY ATTENTION TO THE POWER OF YOUR WORDS.

A careless word may kindle strife;
a cruel word may wreck a life;
a timely word may lessen stress;
a loving word may heal and bless.
—Anonymous

WHEN I WAS a little girl, my mother taught me to respond to other kids' teasing with a cute little poem: "Sticks and stones will break my bones, but names will never hurt me." Mom may have been right about a lot of other stuff, but she was dead wrong about this. Names are powerful. Words are powerful. Choose and use them wisely.

I recall a wonderful sermon I heard some years ago, by Vic Pentz, a Presbyterian pastor who led a small congregation in Southern California. Vic was a handsome guy, with the sturdy physique of an athlete. The way he tugged and pushed at his collar and shoulder indicated that football may have been one of his sports. But on this day the sports tale he told was of wrestling.

When Vic was a teenager, he was overweight, not very tall, and felt terrible about his body. (I must admit, I was comforted, and even a little happy, to hear that women aren't the only ones who have body image problems!) He suffered from low self-esteem, which affected his studies, his dating life (or lack thereof), and his overall level of fulfillment in life. He was not a happy camper.

One day, Vic was in the locker room changing his clothes after wrestling practice and a shower. Around the corner, hidden by a row of lockers, two of the wrestling coaches were talking. Vic couldn't help but overhear what they were saying.

"The guys did good in practice today," the first coach said.

"Yeah, especially Vic," the second coach replied.

"That Vic Pentz, he's as strong as an ox!" the first coach said.

"Yeah, he sure is," the second one replied. Then they continued their conversation about practice and upcoming wrestling matches.

In retelling this story to his congregation many years after the incident, Vic explained how those coaches' words changed his life. In an instant, his low self-regard was skyrocketed to unimagined heights, because of someone else's faith in him. "That Vic Pentz, he's as strong as an ox" became his new mantra. He shrugged off his self-doubts and set about making those words even truer than before. He worked out with weights; he lost weight almost effortlessly; and his self-esteem was transformed. He went on to become a wrestling champion, while maintaining superb academic grades. He took good care of his body, took care of his studies, and graduated with honors. He went on to college, then to divinity school, married, started a family, and became a minister.

Those two coaches never knew that Vic was in the locker room, listening to what they were saying. But their words—just ordinary words—had a huge impact on an insecure teenage boy. They literally changed his life.

But it's not just other people's words that can change lives. Our own words can, too. Have you ever tuned in to listen to yourself while you're talking to someone else? If you're like most people, you might be very surprised to discover how much negativity there is in the words you use in ordinary, day-to-day conversations.

Steve Chandler, author of *100 Ways to Motivate Yourself*, says that within the first few minutes of a conversation, he can tell if the other person thinks like a victim or like an owner. (Chandler's terrific seminar, The Ownership Spirit, is designed to teach people the difference between "victims" and "owners.") I call them "winners" and "whiners."

Whiners say, "I should do *x*."	Winners say, "I want to do *x*."
Whiners say, "These people are driving me crazy."	Winners say, "I control my feelings. I'm not going to let these people get to me."
Whiners say, "I'm swamped. I'll never get all this stuff done."	Winners say, "I'm going to prioritize, then do the important stuff first."
Whiners are reactive.	Winners are proactive.
Whiners say, "This is awful."	Winners say, "How can I make the best of this?"
Whiners say, "I'll never get this right."	Winners say, "This is harder than I thought. I can see I still have a lot to learn."
Whiners focus on blame.	Winners focus on solutions.
Whiners' thought patterns and self-talk lead to fatigue and despair.	Winners' thought patterns and self-talk lead to action.
Whiners think: "How can I get through this?"	Winners think: "What can I get *from* this?"
Whiners feel powerless.	Winners feel personal power.

I could go on and on, but you get the picture. Spend some time listening to other people talk. Can you tell the winners from the whiners?

Now listen to how *you* talk. What are the words you choose to use? How much of your conversation is positive, constructive, life-affirming, and loving? And how much of it is critical, complaining, judging, pessimistic, nay-saying?

Our language reveals our thoughts, feelings, and attitudes.

Whether we are conscious of it or not, our words and our conversations tell others how we see ourselves—and how we see the world. We are constantly revealing who we are by the words we use. If you want to change your self-esteem and your level of self-care, choosing different words is an effective way to do it.

Paying attention to your language and consciously using positive words instead of negative ones is a great habit to develop for a happy life. This is especially true of our self-talk—the silent words in that nonstop conversation that goes on in our heads. As a friend of mine said recently, "If anyone else spoke to me the way I speak to myself, I'd sue them!"

And sometimes such negative self-talk slips out in casual conversation. "I am such a space cadet," I used to say sometimes. I hear other women say far worse: "I am so stupid! How could I have done such a thing?" they scold themselves. "I'll never forgive myself," some women say. Ouch! I wince when I hear that. "Oh, I am so clumsy," a woman in the supermarket said after she dropped a slippery piece of fruit in the produce section.

Let me ask you: Is this kind of self-talk helpful? Or, as Dr. Phil would ask, "How's that workin' for ya?"

I don't know anyone who responds well to self-criticism and harsh self-judgments. It doesn't help you change. It just makes you feel worse about yourself. It makes you believe that you really *are* stupid, clumsy, fat, spacey, an idiot, fill-in-the-blank. Language is powerful. You are what you say you are.

Do you want to know who *I* say you are? I say you are smart, talented, creative, resourceful, kind, loving, generous, lovable, fun, attractive, and a blessing to those who love you. And if you say it, too, day in and day out, sooner or later all of it will be true.

Claim who you are through the words you use. Be the very best *you* that you can be today. Start by watching your language.

PERSONAL CHANGE TIP #5

STICK WITH THE WINNERS. SURROUND YOURSELF WITH THE RIGHT PEOPLE.

No one lives long enough to learn everything they need to learn starting from scratch. To be successful, we absolutely, positively have to find people who have already paid the price to learn the things that we need to learn to achieve our goals.

—Brian Tracy, author of *Eat That Frog!*

YEARS AGO, M. Scott Peck, author of *The Road Less Traveled*, gave a lecture entitled Addiction: The Sacred Disease. During his talk, he pointed out a biblical passage with significant implications for how we go about taking care of ourselves. Peck said: "That famous biblical saying, 'The kingdom of God is within you,' was mistranslated. If you go back to ancient sources and read the sentence in Aramaic (the original language in which it was written), what it really says is: 'The kingdom of God is *among* you.'"

This is *huge*. What it means is that the kingdom of God is in community. We do not find God by going off to the desert alone, or by sitting solitary on a mountaintop, or gazing at our navels 'til we find enlightenment. We find God when we come together with others. "Wherever two or more are gathered, God is there."

We humans are profoundly social creatures. And like other social creatures—monkeys, elephants, lions, porpoises, dogs, parrots, and many more—we were designed to live in relationships with others. We do best when we have a loving, supportive family, clan, tribe, village, town, community, or some other group in which to live and work. We thrive in community—if we isolate, we do so at our own peril.

It has taken me many years to learn this lesson in my own life. I come from a family of Lone Rangers—self-sufficiency was the order of the day. My parents were independent people who believed that it was *not* okay to need others. Borrowing a cup of sugar from a neighbor was seen as "an imposition" and asking for help was a sign of weakness. Mom and Dad, of course, were products of their own upbringing and their culture: The myth of the rugged individual provided the model for how they lived their lives and taught me how to live mine. Our family, like our larger American culture, overemphasizes the individual and underemphasizes relationships and community. As a result, I developed a strong sense that in all things, "I can do it myself."

I grew into a young woman who enthusiastically bought the Superwoman Syndrome hook, line, and sinker. I was convinced I could do it all, have it all, and be it all—all at once! I knew that I was smart, talented, resourceful, and willing to work hard. My schooling reinforced this intense individuality since academic grades are awarded for individual achievement, not group achievement. If you want to be a winner, you do it on your own. Everything in my background taught me to fly solo rather than join groups. "After all," my father sniffed derisively, "eagles don't flock."

Well, Dad, after all these years, I have to tell you, I'm exhausted. Parents sometimes get things wrong, despite their best intentions. And in their admonitions to "do it yourself," my parents were just plain wrong. I figure it this way: If the guys who wrote the Bible could get it wrong about the kingdom of God being within you, I figure my parents can be forgiven for getting it wrong, too.

When it comes to doing the things we know are good for us: If we could have done it by ourselves, we would have done it long ago! The fact that we struggle with taking good care of ourselves tells us that we weren't meant to go it alone—we were meant to do it in relationships, in supportive groups, in community with others.

However, not just any group will do—some groups are composed of people who are committed to being healthy, fulfilled, happy, and successful, while other groups are composed of people who are only interested in commiserating, complaining, and comforting themselves with shared stories of perpetual victimhood and "ain't it awful?" We must choose our companions wisely.

If you're committed to taking good care of yourself, find other people who are already doing it and learn from them. Pick people who have what you want—in terms of attitude and attributes—and do what they do. If you surround yourself with winners, you're more likely to become a winner, too.

In learning how to practice radical self-care, no one can do it for you, but you can't do it alone. The kingdom of God is *among* you.

PERSONAL CHANGE TIP #6

TEACH OTHERS HOW TO DO THE THINGS THEY KNOW ARE GOOD FOR THEM.

We teach best what we most need to learn.

—William James, philosopher, educator

THE MOST POPULAR workshop I teach is called How to Manage Your Boss (and Other Important Relationships). It began as a joke, in the early 1980s. At the time, I had a very difficult boss and was frustrated trying to deal with him. I cried in the ladies' room at work; I lost sleep at night; I complained to friends; I was at my wit's end.

Around this same time, the best-selling business book was *The One Minute Manager*—a wonderful, practical guide to how to get things done through others. One day, my boss's secretary discovered a spoof book entitled *The 59-Second Employee: How to Stay One Significant Second Ahead of Your One-Minute Manager.* She lent me her copy and it was hysterical. After reading, I got what I thought at the time was a brilliant idea.

I decided to offer a class called In Search of an Excellent Boss: The 59-Second Employee—as a joke. I didn't think anyone would really sign up—I just did it to amuse myself and as sort of a mental health exercise. My job was to manage employee training and development at USC—organizing workshops and seminars for the 10,000 employees who worked at the university (faculty, secretaries, financial aid people, food service workers, accountants and other financial folks, program managers, campus security officers, parking attendants, carpenters, plumbers, electricians, and administrators of all types). Each semester I published a catalog, listing all the seminars and workshops available to faculty and staff.

Much to my surprise, when the new catalog came out, with In Search of an Excellent Boss listed as a workshop, over one hundred people signed up! I clearly had hit a nerve with employees all across campus. It was no joke—bad bosses of all stripes were causing problems for the people who worked for them. So I prepared a meaty seminar for workshop participants—and thus was born my most popular class, which I still teach to this day.

The irony is that I was teaching what I most needed to learn myself. Mine was a long, painful history of difficult bosses—each different from the others, but all difficult to work for. If I could teach others how to manage their pain-in-the-ass bosses, perhaps I could teach myself, too.

It worked. Over time, I did get better at managing my bosses. I practiced what I preached, doing my best to use the interpersonal tools I was teaching in my managing your boss workshops.

But I also discovered something important: When I reflected on all the difficult bosses I had had over the years, I asked myself, "What do all those bosses have in common?" The answer was—you guessed it—*me*. I was forced to stop looking at my bosses, and start looking at myself. Could it be that I was a magnet for bad bosses, attracting them into my life, one after the other? Or was it that there was nothing wrong with the bosses—the problem was that I wasn't a very good employee? Oh my. What a surprise that was!

But the truth will set you free. Seeing and acknowledging the truth about ourselves—and accepting it without judgment—is the cornerstone of self-care. In this situation, I acknowledged the fact that I don't like authority figures, especially if they're not very smart or talented. I came to see that I make a terrific team leader, but I'm not a very good team player sometimes, especially if I feel that the team is dragging me down or that I could do a better job than the leader. These and other truths enabled me to see that the best path for me was self-employment.

I've heard it said that "when you work for yourself,

you work for the worst boss of all." I'm not sure that's entirely true, but there's at least a kernel of wisdom there. In self-employment my challenge is managing myself—my attention and focus, my time, my energy, my goals, and my commitments. All of these are essential components of self-care.

So if you want to learn more about how to close the gap between what you know is good for you and what you do about it, teach someone else. Teach your daughters, sisters, nieces, and girlfriends. Teach the women you love how to take really good care of themselves—and in the process, you'll get good at it, too.

Perhaps Richard Bach, author of *Jonathan Livingston Seagull*, says it best: "Learning is finding out what you already know. Doing is demonstrating that you know it. Teaching is reminding others that they know it as well as you do. We are all learners, doers, and teachers."

CONCLUSION

CLOSING THE GAP

You, yourself, as much as anybody in the entire universe, deserve your love and affection.

—The Buddha

MY FRIEND MELISSA Stern took up kayaking when she was sixty-five. She lived near the San Francisco Bay and that's where she took her kayak on Saturdays. One Saturday, Melissa decided to paddle to Angel Island, which is far out in the middle of the bay. As she gazed out over the seemingly endless expanse of waves ahead, her spirits flagged and her confidence sank. "I'll never make it," she thought to herself.

She seriously considered her situation, but kept paddling. Then she got an idea—she took her eyes off Angel Island and instead focused only on the wave right in front of her. Over that wave she paddled, then she took on the next one. Wave by wave, one at a time, Melissa paddled on. Before she knew it, she had arrived at Angel Island.

It seems to me that overcoming the barriers to self-care is not unlike Melissa's kayaking to a distant goal. If we are willing to do things a little differently, a bit at a time, we will make steady progress toward our goals. Simply focus on what's in front of you right now. Don't look too far ahead. Keep paddling, taking one wave at a time. You'll be amazed at how much progress you'll make.

The goal of this book is to help close the gap between what you *know* and what you *do* in terms of taking care of yourself. As you finish the book and find that you have narrowed that gap in your life—even by just one inch—this book has been successful. And so have you.

ABOUT THE AUTHOR

BJ GALLAGHER IS an inspirational author and speaker. She writes business books that educate and empower, women's books that enlighten and entertain, and gift books that inspire and inform. Whether her audience is corporate suits, working women, or the general public, her message is powerful, positive, and practical. She motivates and teaches with empathy, understanding, and more than a little humor.

BJ's international bestseller, *A Peacock in the Land of Penguins* (Berrett-Koehler; third edition 2001), has sold over 300,000 copies in twenty-one languages. Her other books include *Everything I Need to Know I Learned from Other Women* (Conari; 2002), *A True Friend . . . Is Someone Just Like You* (Blue Mountain Arts; 2007), and *YES Lives in the Land of NO* (Berrett-Koehler; 2006).

BJ and her books have been featured on the *CBS Evening News* with Bob Schieffer, the *Today* show with Matt Lauer,

Fox News, PBS, CNN, and other television and radio programs. She is quoted almost weekly in various newspapers, women's magazines, and Web sites, including: *O, The Oprah Magazine*; *Redbook*; *Woman's World*; *Ladies' Home Journal*; *First for Women*; the *New York Times*; the *Chicago Tribune*; the *Wall Street Journal*; the *Christian Science Monitor*; the *Orlando Sentinel*, the *Seattle Post-Intelligencer*, CareerBuilder.com; MSNBC.com; ClubMom.com; and SavvyMiss.com.

In addition to writing books, BJ also conducts seminars and delivers keynotes at conferences and professional meetings across the country. Her corporate clients include IBM, Chevron, John Deere Credit Canada, Volkswagen, Farm Credit Services of America, Raytheon, Marathon Realty (Canada), Chrysler, the *Atlanta Journal-Constitution*, Phoenix Newspapers, Inc., Infiniti, and Nissan.

In Mexico and Colombia, she has taught public seminars on leadership skills for women; here in the United States, she works regularly with chapter presidents and members of the National Assistance League.

BJ is the former manager of training and development for the *Los Angeles Times*, where she was responsible for management development, sales training, customer service seminars, diversity training, specialized programs for women, and the development of high-potential managers.

BJ is a Phi Beta Kappa graduate of the University of Southern California, earning summa cum laude honors with her BA in sociology. She has completed the course work for a PhD in social ethics, also at USC.

For more about BJ Gallagher and her books, visit www.womenneed2know.com.